c. 1

DATE DUE $22.95

DISCARDED

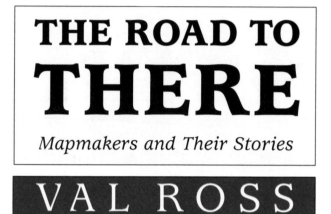

THE ROAD TO
THERE

Mapmakers and Their Stories

VAL ROSS

TUNDRA BOOKS

Published in Canada by Tundra Books,
481 University Avenue, Toronto, Ontario M5G 2E9

Published in the United States by Tundra Books of Northern New York,
P.O. Box 1030, Plattsburgh, New York 12901

Library of Congress Control Number: 2003103802

National Library of Canada Cataloguing in Publication

Ross, Val
    The road to there : mapmakers and their stories / Val Ross.

Includes bibliographical references and index.
ISBN 0-88776-621-8

1. Cartography – History – Juvenile literature.   2. Cartographers – Biography – Juvenile literature.
I. Title.

GA105.6.R68 2003   j912'.09   C2003-901713-3

We acknowledge the financial support of the Government of Canada through the Book Publishing
Industry Development Program (BPIDP) and that of the Government of Ontario through the
Ontario Media Development Corporation's Ontario Book Initiative.

We further acknowledge the support of the Canada Council for the Arts and the Ontario Arts
Council for our publishing program.

Design: Terri Nimmo

Printed and bound in Canada

2 3 4 5 6   08 07 06 05 04

This book is for Jack, who loved to draw maps,
for Erma, who gave me the compass I rely on,
and for the Mappers: Max, Maddie, Zoe,
and of course Morton.

TABLE OF CONTENTS

INVENTING THE ROAD TO THERE

Middle Earth and Mordor exist only in the imagination. That's also where you'll find Lilliput, Treasure Island, Oz, Ruritania, Jurassic Park, and Sim City. You can't walk to these places, yet there are detailed maps of all of them.

When I was young, the medieval-looking maps in C.S. Lewis's Narnia books inspired me to draw geographies of my own private worlds, with cities that went to war and great seas crossed by gallant sailing ships. I drew these maps in colored pencil; now I might use a computer.

There are many kinds of maps: maps that try to represent land according to mathematical principles; simplified diagrams; and descriptions of the landscape in story and song.

But all mapmaking, even the most scientific, involves some degree of imagination. Mapmakers make one country pink, another yellow. They throw a net over the world and call it lines of latitude and longitude. Now mapmakers are trying to tame and name other planets and solar systems.

So maps are more than a means of showing the lines around your property or your country. They give public names to regions that are mysterious. They create the sense that there are routes from Here to There (even if There is in outer space or our own imaginations). They are another way that we can tell stories.

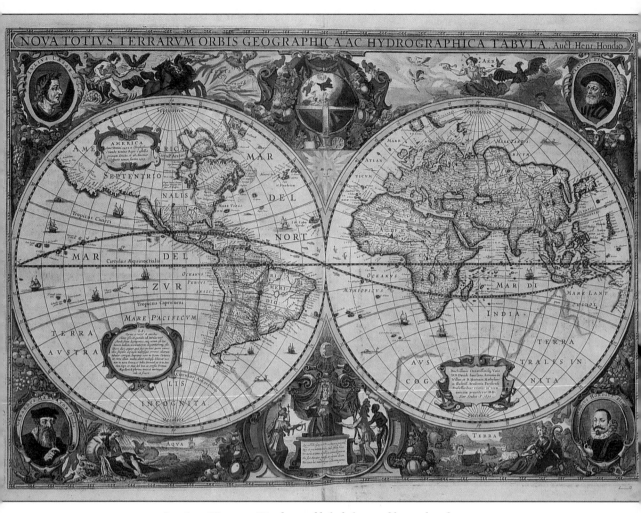

In 1633, *Henricus Hondius published this world map based on the 1595 edition of the Mercator Atlas.*

I

THE MAPMAKER'S SECRET IDENTITY

The Vinland Map

SOME TIME IN the first half of the 20th century, someone picks up a pen and begins to fake an antique map. The forgery will "prove" that the Norsemen, or Vikings, had sailed across the Atlantic Ocean to America long before Christopher Columbus's arrival in 1492.

The forger's pen hovers for a moment above a blank piece of parchment (animal skin prepared as a writing surface). The parchment is no fake. And, although it dates from about 1440 – long after the Norse voyages to "Wineland" or Vinland (the Norse name for North America) around the year 1000 – the forger is not worried, since many mapmakers based their maps on earlier maps. What is important is that his map will seem to predate Columbus.

The forger works carefully, writing in Latin and watering his ink so it will appear faded. He knows that medieval mapmakers used inks mixed from iron compounds that erode and leave a rusty stain, and plans to fake such stains with yellowish dye. He might even add holes to the parchment, to make it look like it was eaten by bookworms.

He draws the Mediterranean Sea, Northern Europe, Iceland, and Greenland. Then he dips his pen again, pauses, and commits himself to making the squiggly line that will turn his map into front-page headlines. Beyond Greenland, he draws a line showing the east coast of North America.

He adds notes to his map. One mentions the discovery of "a new land, extremely fertile and having vines" by the Norseman Leif Eriksson. Another note tells of a journey to Vinland around 1100 by Bishop Eirik Gnupsson of Greenland, who claimed the new land for the Holy Church.

The forger knows a lot about mapmakers of the past. He knows that the first map to use the word "America" was drawn by a German priest named Martin Waldseemüller in 1507. And he knows that any map older than Waldseemüller's that shows North America will be a cartographic bombshell.

The Vinland Map is almost certainly a fake. You can see "Vinlanda" where Baffin Island or Labrador would be, in the upper left. The parchment dates from around 1440, but the ink seems to be from the 20th century.

THE MAPMAKER'S SECRET IDENTITY

In 1957, book dealers tried to sell a "Vinland Map" to the British Museum in London. The map they offered was bound into an old book about an Italian priest's travels to Mongolia. The British Museum experts took a look at the book. They thought the Italian priest part looked genuine. But as for the Vinland Map — they smelled a rat and said, "No, thank you."

So the book dealers decided to unload their Vinland Map in North America. This time, the map convinced people — perhaps because people were ready to be convinced. Scholars had speculated for some time that the Norse had beat Columbus to America because old Icelandic sagas, such as the Greenland Saga and Erik the Red's Saga, described voyages to Vinland around the year 1000. In the late 1950s, archeologists announced that they had found ruins of the Vinland settlement in northern Newfoundland.

North Americans were ready for some hold-in-your-hand proof of the Norse presence in North America. When the book dealers offered the map for sale in North America, a billionaire named Paul Mellon snapped it up for $1 million and donated it to Yale University.

The map was made public in November 1965, just before Columbus Day. This was bad timing for Italian and Spanish Americans who took pride in Columbus, the Italian who had sailed for Spain. They felt it was rude to steal Columbus's thunder, and joined the chorus of English scientists who were already crying "Fake!"

In 1966 the Smithsonian Institution in Washington DC invited experts from all over the world to stop fighting and calmly discuss the map's authenticity. The assembled experts began by questioning the book dealer who sold the map to Paul Mellon. He refused to reveal his sources, but this was not unusual. During World War II, the Nazis had stolen art and book collections from people in countries they conquered. These art

VIKINGS IN VINLAND

Viking poets began to sing the sagas of North American discovery shortly after the year 1000. These heroic poems tell of how warriors led by Bjarni Herjolfsson set off westward from Iceland, checked direction by sighting the stars along their arms, and trusted their single-sail open boats, or knarrs, to get them to Greenland. Instead the winds blew them off course to a new land. From their ships, Bjarni and his men could see tall forests. Fifteen years later, Leif Eriksson followed Bjarni's route and landed with thirty-five colonists. They called the place Vinland because they found fruit – probably Newfoundland's sweet berries – from which they could make wine.

Before long the colonists were attacked by Skraelings – the name the Norse gave to the native Newfoundlanders. One terrible day, Skraelings armed with war clubs killed many Norse. The survivors fled into the forest, but Leif Eriksson's sister Freydis was too pregnant to run. She picked up a sword from one of the dead Norsemen. As the Skraelings moved closer, the sagas say, Freydis bared her breasts and whacked her sword on her body to show that she meant to go down fighting. Rather than mess with this ferocious mother, the Skraelings backed off. When her menfolk returned, Freydis mocked them for being cowards.

The Norse colony in Vinland didn't last long. The Skraelings kept attacking. And Freydis, greedy for the possessions of her fellow colonists, axe-murdered some of them. Finally, say the sagas, the survivors returned to Iceland and told their stories. About 200 years later, when Icelanders learned to read and write, these sagas were written down – with "maps" of Vinland hidden in their poetry.

objects found their way to dealers after the war. Dealers were reluctant to reveal too much about where their treasures came from, in case the original owners reclaimed them. All the Vinland Map conference could get from the book dealer was that he had acquired the map from "a private European collector."

Then the experts discussed how the strange map was found, bound into an old book. Bookbinding experts ran their fingers over the object and put their noses down to literally sniff it. They decided that the binding that attached the book and the map was suspiciously new, possibly even from the early 20th century. Even more puzzling, the Vinland Map wormholes didn't match the wormholes in the book's other pages. How could worms stop dead at one page and resume burrowing in a new direction on the next?

The map's defenders had answers for both these objections: Maybe the book's pages fell out and got mixed up. Maybe the book was rebound in the early 20th century.

Everyone at the conference spent a surprising amount of time discussing wormholes — because by the early 20th century, antique maps were starting to be worth real money. For example, in 1901, you could have bought a 1482 edition of Ptolemy's *Cosmographia* for $350. In 1950, the asking price was $5,000. By 1965, the year before the Vinland Map Conference, it was priced at $28,000. As old maps gained value, forgers learned how to make maps look older by faking wormholes, sometimes drilling them with hot wires. One Yale professor said he knew of an English bookseller who kept "a stable of live worms," to munch up modern maps so they would appear ancient.

Since the experts couldn't resolve the worm question, they turned to the map's contents. Many were very suspicious that the Vinland Map showed Greenland as an island. European sailors didn't know that for sure until the late 19th century. "No problem," said the map's defenders.

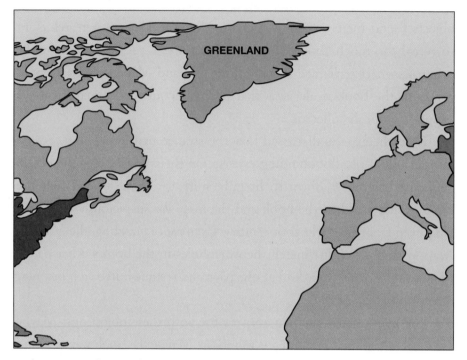

Today's map of the area shown in the Vinland Map.

If the map had been drawn by Bishop Eirik of Greenland, he might have made Greenland an island because it was easier to claim islands for the Church than whole continents.

The scientists heard reports on the map's ink crusts, and whether the ink was flaking the way old crusts of ink should flake. They examined the map under ultraviolet light. But when the conference broke up after two days of intense talk, the Vinland Map mystery remained unsolved.

Years passed. Some people who believed in the map estimated that, if it was genuine, it would be worth about $25 million.

But not everyone believed in it. In 1974, a Chicago scientist analyzing its ink and the yellowish stains detected the presence of round, whitish crystals. He identified them as anatase, a chemical compound not in use until the 1920s. He said the map was a fraud. Other chemists speculated that the anatase might have somehow settled on the map during its handling by modern scientists. They said that the Vinland Map could still be real.

In 1995, American scientists completed a seven-year-long radiocarbon study of the parchment the map was drawn on. They pinned down its age to the year 1434; the parchment, at least, was genuine. Then chemists from the University of London aimed a laser at the map's ink and its stains, and detected anatase in the actual pigment itself.

Now most experts agree that the parchment is old, but what's drawn on it is new. So much for the Vinland Map's $25-million value. (A few diehards still insist the thing could be genuine, though, and Yale University is hanging on to it.)

This Babylonian map, made in the 6th century B.C. on a clay tablet, is the oldest map still in existence that attempts to show a view of the whole world. This "world" has the city of Babylon (in modern Iraq) in the middle. The Earth is circular and is surrounded by seas.

But who made it and why?

In 2002, an American historian named Kirsten Seaver came forward with a plausible theory about the Vinland Map's forger. She named a Jesuit priest, Father Josef Fischer.

Many map dealers and scholars knew that name well. In fact, it was Father Fischer who had found Martin Waldseemüller's 1507 book on geography, in which he explained why he thought the New World should be named "America." As a scholar of early mapmaking, Father Fischer had access to old libraries where he could have found a blank piece of parchment. But if he had the knowledge, the connections, and the skills to commit the forgery, what was his motive?

Kirsten Seaver says that in the late 1930s the old priest was living in retirement in an Austrian monastery. Then the Nazis took it over and decided to shut it down. Furious, Father Fischer decided to forge a map that would embarrass them.

He knew that the Nazis refuted Christianity, and that they had bizarre ideas about the superiority of the illiterate, primitive Norse people, regarding them as the "master race." Father Fischer gambled that the Nazis would champion his fake map because they hungered for anything that showed what heroes the Norse were. But, in championing the map, the Nazis would be forced to publicize the text on the map — including the "fact" that the New World had been claimed by a Christian, the bishop of Greenland. It was all there on the same document. If they accepted one part, they had to accept the other.

The jury is still out on Seaver's solution to the mystery of the Vinland Map and who made it. But the fact that it was forged, acquired a huge value, and was taken seriously, reveals some of our feelings about maps.

Maps have authority. They make claims, stake out territory, and confirm history. We decide that they are worth huge amounts of money when they tell us the history that we want to hear.

THE MAPMAKER'S SECRET IDENTITY

The people who originally composed the Vinland sagas did not record things by writing them down, and the history most of us learn doesn't usually give credit to pre-literate peoples for their land claims. We are used to reserving our respect for documents and charts. The sagas, and the Vinland Map, are reminders that maps can come in many forms, and so can mapmakers. The story of the Vinland Map is also proof that the best way to read a map is to learn what you can about the mapmakers, and figure out what they were really trying to show you.

Only then are you ready to find your own way.

THE MAPMAKER'S BEST FRIEND

King Roger II and Al-Idrisi

IT IS THE year 1145, and two men stare down at a drawing table in the royal palace of the kingdom of Sicily, amid the hot scent of lemon and orange groves. They are an unlikely pair. One is the large, hoarse-voiced king of Sicily, a Christian. The other man is a diplomatic, gentle-voiced scholar from North Africa, and a Muslim.

Although it is the time of the first Crusades, when Christian knights and Muslim warriors are hacking each other to pieces in the Holy Land, the king and the scholar are friends. The king gives money and support, gathering information from travelers, traders, and pilgrims. The Muslim is using this research to create the greatest map of the 12th century.

The king, Roger de Hauteville, born in 1095, was the grandson of Norman warlords, descendants of Norsemen who had wandered into Italy looking for things to steal and people to kill. Unlike the Normans who invaded England in 1066, these southern Normans quickly realized they could get a better grip on power, not by crushing the cultures of the people they had defeated, but by working with them and learning from them. In Sicily, the de Hautevilles joined

Christians and Muslims into a society that, for a few shining years, was the most multicultural, educated, and tolerant in Europe.

Roger II was almost five years old, studying under Greek and Muslim tutors in the palace at Palermo, when the man who would become his best friend was born in the Muslim city of Ceuta, at the western end of the Mediterranean. The boy was named (take a deep breath) Abu Abdullah Mohammed ibn-Muhammed ibn-Abdallah ibn-Idris al-Sharif al-Idrisi (sometimes it's "Edrisi" or "Edris"). *Al-Sharif* means "the noble"; unlike Roger's family, al-Idrisi's ancestors were true aristocrats, descendants of the Caliphs who ruled Malaga in Spain.

Set up almost like a comic strip, this illuminated manuscript shows important events in Roger's life, including his three marriages and his coronation as King of Sicily.

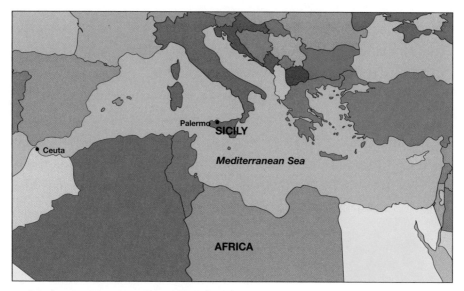

Today's map of Roger's Sicily and al-Idrisi's Africa.

Al-Idrisi's schooling was even better than Roger's. He studied at the university in Cordoba, Spain. Then, like some hippie from the 1960s, he traveled Europe and North Africa, writing poetry. Perhaps al-Idrisi was also on the run from political rivals back home. In any case, he accepted a strange invitation that came his way in the year 1138 from the newly crowned Christian king of Sicily, Roger II. Al-Idrisi might have heard that this Roger was not like other Christians; he wanted to expand not only his empire but also his mind. Roger's court was becoming famous as a place where doctors, mathematicians, astrologers, and poets — many of them Muslim — held debates in the pleasure gardens and wrote in the shade of Roger's stone courtyards.

Did Roger want al-Idrisi's advice on expanding his power into Muslim lands? At its closest point, Sicily is only 150 kilometers (90 miles) from North Africa. Roger knew that whoever wanted to master the central Mediterranean Sea and its trade had to control that southern coast — and control the Muslim princes who were always plotting to win

THE MAPMAKER'S BEST FRIEND

back the orange and lemon groves of Sicily that the Normans had so recently captured from them.

Just three years before al-Idrisi arrived in Sicily, ambassadors from Byzantium and Venice complained to the Holy Roman Emperor about Roger. The Byzantines and Venetians wanted Roger to leave Africa to its "rightful" rulers — the other Christians. They mistrusted the Sicilian king: he spoke Arabic and, after capturing Muslim towns, usually let his Muslim subjects have their own courts of law and the freedom to practice their own religion. Roger just didn't act like a good Christian. Look at how he behaved when Baldwin, the Norman king of Jerusalem, sent emissaries to Sicily to beg Roger to conquer a North African kingdom and convert it. Roger's Christian warriors urged the king to act on this splendid idea. But Ibn al-Athir, an Arab who wrote a history of Roger's court, tells us that the king lifted his foot and farted, and then told his knights, "By my faith, here is better counsel than you give."

Other Christian rulers thought Roger showed too much respect for Muslims. When al-Idrisi arrived at the Sicilian court, as a sign of extra courtesy and favor, he was allowed to ride a mule into Roger's presence. The king, crowned in Byzantine-style with pendant pearls hanging down to his shoulders, stepped down from his throne and went forward to greet his guest. Muslim historians of Roger's court tell us that, before long, al-Idrisi was seated beside the king, where he could whisper in Roger's ear.

Some of their conversations were more public. Ibn al-Athir tells the story of how news arrived one day that Roger's expedition took the Muslim city of Tripoli and killed many Muslim defenders. The Christian knights cheered but al-Idrisi, seated at the king's side, showed no emotion. Roger turned to his friend and demanded, "Where was your god? Has he forgotten his people?" Al-Idrisi boldly replied, "If my God was far away, he was taking part in the capture of Edessa, which has just been taken by the Muslims from the Christians." The Christian knights jeered and yelled. But the king said, "By God, do not laugh at him! This man always speaks the truth."

Indeed, the Christian king and his Muslim scholar-friend were so close, Sicilians gossiped that Roger had secretly converted to Islam. But the true basis of their friendship was that they were working together on Roger's grand project: the world's most beautiful and accurate map. It was to be made of silver, engraved with outlines of coasts and islands.

They started, as most medieval mapmakers did, with the writings of Claudius Ptolemy, the ancient Greek-Egyptian. But they weren't content to repeat his observations — or his errors. Al-Idrisi's own writings say that he and Roger also consulted Muslim geographers such as Ibn-Hawqal, who had visited Palermo around 872. After carrying out what al-Idrisi calls "an exhaustive and detailed investigation" of such geographical classics, the two mapmakers decided to launch their own independent inquiry.

All of Claudius Ptolemy's original maps are lost, but many later mapmakers tried to reconstruct them according to directions in his writings. This is from a German edition of the Cosmographia *published more than 1,100 years after Ptolemy's death.*

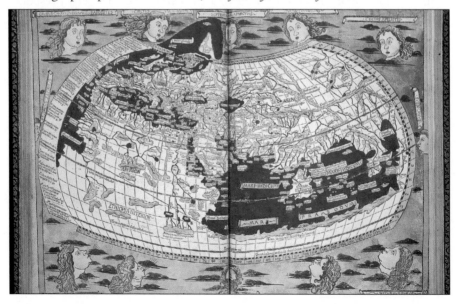

THE MAPMAKER'S BEST FRIEND

PTOLEMY

Claudius Ptolemy, a Greek living in Egypt, influenced mapmaking from his own lifetime (around 150 AD) until about 1500. His insights were more useful, and his mistakes more damaging, than any other ancient scientist. His maps had all disappeared by the Middle Ages, but some of his books survived.

One of his greatest works was his *Geographia*. This book explained scale – that is, showing distance and area accurately by having a large measure of distance equal a tiny measure of length on the map. Ptolemy told how the world could be divided into zones, or latitudes – from zones near the equator with a hot climate and 12 hours of daylight all year round, right up to the highest latitudes with a frigid climate and very short winter days. He explained that a grid of lines, running from north to south and east to west across the world, would let people reading maps locate any place, anywhere. Helpfully, Ptolemy even listed 8,000 places, with their coordinates, which later mapmakers consulted when they were drawing up their charts of the world.

Unfortunately, Ptolemy's two biggest errors held back science for more than 1,400 years. He was convinced that the Earth was the center of the Solar System and everything revolved around it. And he insisted that the Earth consisted mostly of land surrounding the vast Mediterranean Sea. It was not until the 1540s that Gerard Mercator finally cut Ptolemy's Mediterranean down to size, and the astronomer Copernicus showed that the Earth revolves around the sun.

The king ordered "experienced travelers"– sailors, traders, pilgrims – to come from all over his kingdom to Palermo for questioning. Then he and al-Idrisi compared these fresh reports with existing maps and, using an iron compass, sketched maps on a massive drawing board.

After years of research, the two were ready to proceed with the ultimate map. Another Muslim historian, al-Safadi, wrote that the king had 400,000 drams of silver brought to al-Idrisi, who ordered silversmiths to turn it into a silver sphere "like those in the heavens." Roger was so pleased that, although his friend used only a third of the silver, the king told him to keep the rest.

The large, flat map, or planisphere, measured about 3.5 x 1.5 meters (11 x 5 feet) and weighed about 180 kilograms (400 pounds). But what this glittering object was made of was less precious than what was engraved on its surface – the outlines of the known world.

South is at the top of al-Idrisi's world map; turn it upside down and suddenly you recognize the Mediterranean and Black Seas, and even Arabia.

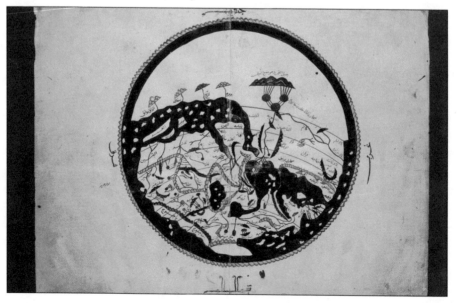

There are many problems with al-Idrisi's vision of the world. England is just a tiny blip floating off the coast of Europe. And Africa reaches to Antarctica – you cannot get to India by sailing around it. But the mapmakers got the Nile River right. The map shows how the Blue Nile flows from Ethiopia, and the White Nile flows from the Mountains of the Moon in central Africa (something British geographers didn't confirm until the middle of the 19th century). The map even sketches in Scandinavia and Japan. Like the ancient Greek geographers, al-Idrisi believed that the Earth was round, and calculated its circumference to be about 37,000 kilometers (23,000 miles) – it's actually more like 40,000 kilometers (25,000 miles).

The planisphere wasn't as sophisticated as Chinese maps of the time. But al-Idrisi was way ahead of the mapmakers of northern Europe, who were more concerned with showing the way to heaven than depicting the outlines of the Earth.

Al-Idrisi wrote a book to accompany his planisphere – *Nuzhat al-Mushtaq fi'khtiraq al-afar* (*The Book of Pleasant Journeys into Faraway Lands*). Better known as *The Book of Roger*, it is an encyclopedia of information about the peoples of the known world, "their seas, mountains and measurements . . . crops, revenues and all sorts of buildings . . . and all the wonderful things relating to each."

Again, the hardworking mapmakers got some things marvelously wrong. On the island of Wak-Wak, they report, trees grew talking fruits shaped like women's heads; all day, these fruits called out "Wak Wak!" *The Book of Roger* reported that the people of Norway were born neckless, and that "England is set in the Ocean of Darkness . . . in the grip of perpetual winter."

After fifteen years of labor, in January 1154, al-Idrisi announced that the silver map and book were finally complete. But by now Roger was an old man. He died later that same year.

Within six years his kingdom began to fall apart. Roger's heir, King William the Bad, was no Roger. After his father's death, William couldn't defend Roger's African conquests, so cities such as Tripoli slipped back into Muslim hands. Thousands of Christians fled back to Sicily, where William hadn't paid much attention to ruling.

ANCIENT MAPS

The Romans worked on maps that tried to portray the world to scale, but none of them survive. What do survive are cartograms, maps in which the land is distorted to show how to get from A to B, for use by their armies and traders. One of these, the Peutinger Map, shows towns in the order in which you'd reach them as you marched along a Roman road. There are hardly any twists or curves, and Europe and the Near East are shown as if they are parallel, like guitar strings.

After the Roman Empire fell and life in the West became violent and chaotic, mapmakers made maps that drastically simplified their world. These maps were mainly diagrams to help people on the journey to heaven. Most were in what's known as the T-O design. Earth was a circle (the O) divided into three parts by a T of water – the Mediterranean, the Nile, and the Danube River. The holy city of Jerusalem is shown at the center of the world. Asia or the Orient is on top (which is why we say we "get oriented" when we find direction). Europe is on the left and Africa is on the right.

The monks who made these maps gave them amazing decorations. So, on many maps from the Middle Ages, you can't recognize the shapes of continents, but you can see saints, mermaids, and monsters.

On the morning of March 9, 1161, rebels stormed the palace, threw open the dungeons, and armed the prisoners. William and his family were put under guard. A mob from the streets of Palermo swarmed over the palace like locusts. Muslim scholars were hunted down in the halls and killed. Rioters started throwing books, documents, and tax records into a bonfire in the courtyard. Anything of value was carried away. The great silver planisphere engraved with a map of the world disappeared that day, and was never seen again.

What was also lost in Sicily that day was the idea of a kingdom where people of different faiths could live, debate, and study in peace. Roger's son and his family survived the riots and regained control over Sicily — but they turned their attention to staying secure inside their walls. Across Europe it was the same. The best minds of the Middle Ages closed against the outside world. People who wondered about what lay beyond their own horizons risked being condemned as heretics. Mapmaking turned into a question of how to portray the world to prove the supremacy of Christianity, and how many monsters you could draw to cover the blank spots that made up most of the map.

Luckily the rioters did not destroy al-Idrisi's other major work, *The Book of Roger*, with its draft maps. In fact, King William commissioned another book, *Gardens of Pleasure and Recreation of the Souls*, from his father's old friend. After writing it, al-Idrisi went home to Ceuta and grieved for Roger, his Christian friend who once shared his desire to understand the world. "The extent of his learning cannot be described," al-Idrisi wrote, "so deeply and wisely has he studied. . . . His dreams are worth more than the waking thoughts of most mortals." As al-Idrisi knew, a mapmaker's best friend is someone who is interested in the stories his maps have to tell.

3

THE MAPMAKER'S LOSS

Cheng Ho

THE BOY IS about ten years old when rebels sweep into China's Yunnan province, killing anyone connected to the hated Mongols who have occupied China for 200 years. The boy's father, a Muslim whose family governed Yunnan for the Mongols, is executed along with thousands of others. The boy is taken prisoner and castrated – cut, the way we "fix" male cats and dogs – so that he can never have children.

But his captors notice that the boy is clever and handsome. "His eyebrows were like swords and his forehead was like a tiger's," a Chinese court official later writes. And so he is given to the new Chinese emperor's fourth son, Prince Zhu Di. The Prince educates the boy and gives him a Chinese name, Cheng Ho (the historical form of Zheng Ho or Zheng He), and a title, San Bao (Three Jewels).

The story of Cheng Ho's life seems like a fairytale – the orphan boy grows up to be the Prince's most trusted advisor. But the real story is even more exciting.

When Prince Zhu Di's father, the rebel-turned-emperor, died in 1398, his throne passed to his grandson, Zhu Yunwen. Zhu Di mistrusted his nephew, with good reason. The new emperor immediately started eliminating any uncles who might claim the throne. Zhu Di decided to kill before he was killed. His loyal servant Cheng Ho, now in his early twenties, was at his side as he started his own rebellion. In 1402, Zhu Di's army marched into Nanjing, hunting for the Emperor. They found his imperial palace in flames, and inside, the charred bodies of the empress, her son, and someone else. Was it Emperor Zhu Yunwen? The body was too blackened to tell.

Prince Zhu Di claimed China's throne. But he was unsure that the man he had stolen it from was really dead. Some said the deposed emperor had fled the burning palace in disguise and was hiding in some foreign country.

This pictorial map of the Yellow River, the Huang He Wan Li Tu, was about the size and shape of the red carpet at an awards show. Created by ten of China's most famous artists around 1368, just before the time of Cheng Ho, it is not only beautiful, but useful: each house represents a hundred families, so the map could be used to assess the damage whenever the Yellow River flooded.

So the new emperor, Zhu Di, put Cheng Ho in command of ships that would search the world for traces of Zhu Yunwen.

Emperor Zhu Di had many reasons for creating a mighty fleet of ships. Years of fighting the Mongols, followed by civil war, had ruined China's economy. Pirates grew rich on stolen cargo meant for China's markets. The kingdom was running short of spices and medicinal herbs. Trade had to be reopened. There was another reason: because Emperor Zhu Di was the grandson of a rebel peasant, and because he himself had

SAILING IN OLD CHINA

Cheng Ho's ships were centuries ahead of European vessels in terms of sailing technology. They had floating anchors at each side to stabilize the ship in high seas, and watertight compartments so that a leak in one part would not sink the whole ship – something the designers of the Titanic should have copied 500 years later. Their square sails of red silk could be adjusted so that they could sail on days when the European-designed ships waited for the wind to change direction. The biggest ships of the Treasure Fleet had nine masts and were 120 meters (400 feet) long – among the biggest wooden vessels ever to have been built. They were like floating towns, with gardens of potted plants and pens of livestock to provide food for their crews.

Even 600 years ago, Chinese sailors used compasses to navigate. In fact, the Chinese probably invented the compass – they used magnetized needles floating in stone bowls to help sailors find north even in fog or on starless nights.

THE MAPMAKER'S LOSS

stolen the throne, he felt he had to impress the world that he was a true ruler. He wanted his Ming dynasty to claim its place among the great periods of China's past, when China's ships dominated the China Sea.

Zhu Di knew he had put the right man in charge of the Treasure Fleet. Most Chinese were followers of the great teacher Confucius, who taught respect and serenity, and discouraged curiosity about distant lands. But Cheng Ho was a Muslim, whose faith encouraged him to travel and spread the word of Allah. Muslims had been running China's trade with Persia and Arabia for centuries.

We know of Cheng Ho's adventures through the writings of Ma Huan, another Muslim who served as a translator on the later voyages and wrote an account of his travels, *The Overall Survey of the Ocean's Shores*. "I am but a stupid, incompetent driveler," wrote Ma Huan, "but in the discharge of my work with Cheng Ho, I candidly and honestly set down many strange things." Ma Huan's stories aren't at all like the histories of the European explorers who would later rampage through the civilizations of other lands, conquering and looting. Ma Huan tells of diplomacy and courtesy, and of the world paying tribute to China's Emperor.

The first time the Treasure Fleet set sail was in the golden autumn of 1405. As 217 great, red-sailed vessels passed down the Chinese coast, their mere presence proclaimed that China was once again in charge of the seas.

Cheng Ho's fleet made diplomatic calls in Java, Sumatra, Sri Lanka, Kerala, and southwest India, a trading center for jewels and ginger, pepper, cinnamon, and cardamom. Heading for home, the ships dropped their mighty anchors at Palembang in Sumatra, headquarters of the strongest pirate chief in Southeast Asia. Here, says Ma Huan, Cheng Ho's sailors did battle, killing 5,000 pirates and taking the pirate chief back to Nanjing to be beheaded in front of the Emperor.

Back in China, thousands were dying from epidemics. In 1407 the ships sailed forth again, carrying 180 doctors and pharmacists. The

Chinese healers were ordered to bring back medicines such as sulfur (for lung problems) and chaulmoogra oil (for leprosy), and to consult with Arab doctors, who were at that time the best doctors in the world.

Once more the ships returned after about two years, laden with medicines, spices, gems, and foreign ambassadors bearing gifts for Emperor Zhu Di. The foreign ambassadors were welcomed with banquets of duck and horse, fried and steamed pancakes, sweet bean paste and plum wine. Then they were sent back to their homelands, carrying gifts of silk, brocade, and porcelain.

But by now, Emperor Zhu Di's bureaucrats were questioning the cost of the voyages. He ignored them. More fleets sailed out and returned with tribute — and no sign of Zhu Di's vanished nephew. The Emperor

Admiral Cheng Ho is shown in full Ming dynasty regalia on this stamp from the Republic of China. There are statues of the great navigator, but no portraits made in his lifetime, so this is just an artist's impression.

The biggest ships in the Treasure Fleet were eight times bigger than the ships sailed by Christopher Columbus, and were better designed for long sea voyages than European ships would be until the mid-18th century.

This stamp shows the Hong Kong portion of the long, scrolled Mao K'un map, which is described as "a memento of Cheng Ho's achievements."

THE MAPMAKER'S LOSS

began to feel confident, and in 1416 he ordered this inscription to be made in a temple: "The seas had been conquered and there was quiet in the four corners."

Ma Huan joined the Treasure Fleet for its fourth and fifth voyages. These later expeditions were smaller, but sailed farther west than before, to Arabia. Ma Huan described it as a place where "the women all wear a covering over their heads" and everyone spoke "the Al-a-pi" (Arabic) language.

After Arabia, the great red sails turned to Malindi, Africa, for exotic animals. Cheng Ho knew that the king of Bengal had sent the Emperor a giraffe, and the animal was hailed as the "qilin" — a mythical creature believed to appear only in times of great prosperity. So, to please Zhu Di, Cheng Ho brought home a second giraffe/qilin. When it was presented to the court, a poet wrote that the miraculous creature had "luminous spots like a red cloud or purple mist. . . . It walks in stately fashion. . . . The manifestation of its divine spirit rises up to heaven."

The appearance of another qilin convinced the Emperor that the omens were good for his other grand project, moving China's capital to Beijing. Just as China's Treasure Fleet was dazzling the world, so her new Forbidden City would command awe from all the lesser nations.

But the cost of building the new court at the Forbidden City, and of mounting the voyages of the Treasure Fleet, was seriously straining China's finances. Cheng Ho's sixth voyage consisted of a mere forty-one ships. They left Nanjing in 1421, mostly to carry foreign dignitaries back to their native lands. Cheng Ho probably didn't even go the whole way, because court records show that he attended the celebrations for the new Forbidden City. Perhaps he wanted to be close to his master to protect him from impending disaster.

The Emperor's projects were costing China dearly at a time of epidemics, famines in the north, and rebellions in the south. In the spring

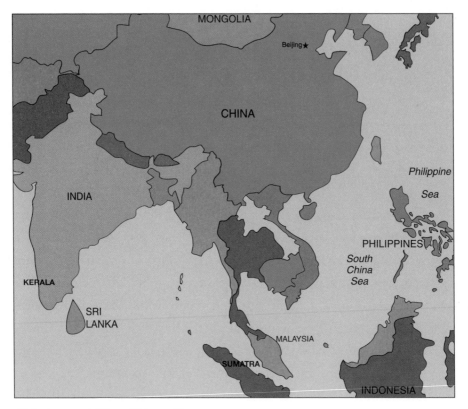

Today's map of Cheng Ho's world.

of 1421 Zhu Di was thrown from his horse. Then lightning struck three gold-roofed halls of the new palace, and they collapsed in flames. These were very bad omens. Yet, against the advice of his counselors, Zhu Di launched a costly military campaign against the northern Mongols and sent Cheng Ho south to Sumatra to solve a local dispute there.

Cheng Ho was away when the Emperor died in the summer of 1424, and he returned to find Zhu Di's extremely Confucian son on the throne. Just a month after Zhu Di's death, in September 1424, the new Emperor issued an edict: "All voyages of the Treasure Ships are to be stopped." The welfare of the new emperor's starving subjects was more important than showing off in front of barbarians.

THE MAPMAKER'S LOSS

But this emperor reigned for only a short time and was succeeded by Zhu Di's grandson, Zhu Zhanji, who seemed to be more like Cheng Ho's old master. In 1430, concerned by the way China's trade and payments from overseas were drying up, Zhu Zhanji began to talk of another voyage, and sent for retired admiral Cheng Ho. The old man must have encouraged him, for Zhu Zhanji ordered the biggest fleet ever – 300 ships and 27,500 men.

Once more, in 1431, a mighty red-sailed fleet journeyed into the China Sea. Ma Huan tells us that the fleet stopped in Vietnam, Java, and Sumatra. Other reports hint that the ships sailed all the way to Australia. On the voyage home, Cheng Ho died at age sixty-two.

When the ships reached home, they unloaded many treasures, including another giraffe/qilin. This one failed to impress Emperor Zhu Zhanji, who was turning out to be a proper Confucian after all. To the

CHENG HO IN AUSTRALIA?

In 1879, road crews working near Darwin, Australia, made a strange discovery. A small statuette from the Ming period was found tangled in the roots of a great banyan tree, which over centuries had grown around it. The statue is of Shu Lao, a Taoist immortal, seated on a deer and holding a peach (a symbol of long life). Of the many pieces of Chinese porcelain found along Australia's north coast, this was one of the oldest and most intact; it was probably placed there, rather than washed ashore from a shipwreck. Was the statue dropped by traders? Or did Cheng Ho's sailors reach Australia centuries before Europeans? We don't know.

relief of his people, he announced, "I do not care for foreign things."

And so in the year 1433, a generation before the birth of Christopher Columbus, the Emperor of China shut the door on the outside world. By 1500, when greedy European eyes were lighting up at the prospect of gold-rich kingdoms in the Americas, China passed a law forbidding the

THE MAO K'UN CHART

The Beijing bureaucrats didn't burn all of Cheng Ho's charts. One survives in the Wu Pei Chi, or "Records for Military Preparations," a manual written in 1621.

Known as the Mao K'un chart, it is painted on a scroll 508 cm (200 inches) long and 20 cm (8 inches) wide, but it may have been cut down from an even longer scroll. It doesn't show a bird's-eye view of a coastline, but instead depicts an irregular line of mountains along the horizon, like the view from a passing ship. Its scale varies, showing densely populated cities on a larger scale than long stretches of countryside.

The chart is covered with useful bits of sailing advice. To navigate Singapore Strait, for example, the text advises, "From Little Karimun Island at 103 degrees, 24 minutes east, sail for 5 watches. . . ." Each day was divided into ten "watches" of 2.4 hours, and sailors kept track of the length of a watch by noting how long it took to burn specially marked sticks of incense. For nighttime navigation, the chart contained instructions for sailing by the stars, including notes on how many "fingers" above the horizon each star should be. In all, the Mao K'un chart lists about 300 places outside China and is the first Chinese map to try to represent southeast Asia.

construction of sea-going ships on pain of death. In 1551, thirty years after Ferdinand Magellan's ships crossed the Pacific, the Ming dynasty rulers made it a crime of "espionage" to even go to sea in a boat with more than one mast.

Although Cheng Ho died an honored man, after his death his accomplishments were hushed up. One court adviser said that Zhu Di's Treasure Fleet was an example of bad government. Another official burned most of Cheng Ho's documents, calling them exaggerations. By the mid-15th century, there was nobody left in China capable of constructing giant, seaworthy ships. China went to sleep just as Europe was awakening and feeling hungry.

So what did Cheng Ho accomplish? He didn't "discover" anywhere new; he visited places already known to Arab and Chinese traders. Although Chinese mapmaking was highly sophisticated, Cheng Ho's charts are not a breakthrough in terms of cartography. You make the maps you need, and Cheng Ho's were about making safe but impressive entrances in front of new people.

Cheng Ho is one of history's great might-have-beens. When he sailed between 1405 and 1433, it was more likely that the world would be mapped by China than by a handful of puny, primitive European kingdoms. Had China's rulers used the skills and information Cheng Ho brought back from his great voyages, the people who colonized the world would have come not from Europe but from China. And you wouldn't be reading this book in English but in Mandarin Chinese.

Cheng Ho's tragedy is that he was cut off by the Ming rulers in two ways. Not only could he have no children, his work was inherited by no one — because Ming laws forbade it.

But he is not completely forgotten. There are islands off Africa where the people's skin is more golden than that of other Africans, and where the local legends speak of ancestors arriving in huge ships. Chinese communities in Indonesia still honor the legendary figure of San Bao. There is a temple to him in Malacca. And some say that "San Bao the sailor" sounds like "Sinbad the Sailor" from the *Arabian Nights*. Sinbad's story begins, "I have seen oceans where the sun rises" and continues, "I have traded fabric for ginger and camphor . . . ivory and pearls."

If Cheng Ho is Sinbad the Sailor, his story is more than a fairytale. It is an inspiring record of accomplishment and diplomacy. But it is also a terrible lesson of loss. No matter how far you go, no matter how brave and skilled you are, you still need to come home to people who care about your stories and your maps.

THE MAPMAKER'S BROTHERS

Henry the Navigator

IT IS EARLY morning, August 8, 1444, and people are gathering in a field outside Lagos, a town in Portugal in southern Europe, to see something they have never seen before. Sailors are dragging dark-skinned men, women, and children from Africa into the field. This terrible morning is the first slave market, the beginning of the European slave trade.

The 15th-century chronicler Gomes Eannes de Zurara writes about that day. Some of the captives stare down at the earth, he reports, while others, "faces bathed in tears," look towards the sky for help. As the Portuguese begin to separate the captives so that they can be sold, "Mothers clasped their infants in their arms and threw themselves on the ground to cover them with their bodies . . . so that they could prevent their children from being separated from them."

Watching this scene is a man dressed in dark clothes astride a powerful horse. He is Dom Enrique, third son of Joao, King of Portugal, but he is known in history books as Prince Henry the Navigator. He is a strict Christian and, in his twisted logic, he is doing the Africans a favor. If they had been captured by Muslim slave traders, they would have been converted to Islam. But as captives of the Portuguese, they will become Christians. Zurara says that Prince Henry finds it very satisfying "to contemplate the salvation of those souls."

The obsessive curiosity that turns people into explorers and mapmakers can open new horizons – or lead them to exploit and betray. Probably Prince Henry doesn't feel shame about introducing the slave trade to Europe. He will die proud of his accomplishments: the expansion of Portugal's glory, the conversion of Africans to be his brothers in Christ, the discovery and mapping of new lands. Perhaps he does not even think about his own royal brothers, two of whom he will leave to die early deaths.

Prince Henry came from a family that was a medieval nightmare. His grandfather, Prince Pedro, had fallen in love with a lady-in-waiting, Ines de Castro. Pedro's father, the king, disapproved and had Ines executed. When Pedro became king, he ordered that Ines's executioners should have their hearts ripped out. Then he had Ines's corpse dug up, and forced his courtiers to kiss her cold, dead hand.

When you marry into a family that is so haunted by bad memories, you try hard to bring up your children to be extra good. King Pedro's son Joao married a very proper English lady, Philippa of Lancaster, who took religion very seriously. Queen Philippa "found the court a sink of immorality; she left it chaste as a nunnery" wrote one Portuguese historian. In 1415, on her deathbed, the Queen summoned her sons to her side. Little Prince Fernando was too young, but Duarte (Edward), Pedro (Peter), and Enrique (Henry) came and were given specially forged swords with hilts of gold and pearls. Philippa made her boys swear to be chivalrous knights, and stay loyal to each other. Each brother promised – and Henry promised himself that he would make his mother proud by never marrying, and by being particularly religious.

The Queen had one more request. She told her princes to cleanse their hands of the Christian blood that had been shed in Portugal's civil wars by "washing in the blood of the infidel" – the Muslims of North Africa. As she closed her eyes, they told her they were preparing to launch a secret attack on the Muslim city of Ceuta just across the Straits of Gibraltar. If they won Ceuta, they would also gain trade with countries all over the Mediterranean, an opportunity to seize the riches of Africa and maybe find a route to India.

On August 20, 1415, as darkness fell, the Portuguese attacked Ceuta, hometown of the great Arab mapmaker al-Idrisi. Henry was among those leading the charge. The invaders soon breached the walls, and – under cover from English archers – took the city by the next day. The capture of Ceuta was the start of Henry's crusade to bring Africa under the sign of the Christian cross and to get rich by doing so. He did not realize that, in fulfilling his project, he would help replace the old Christian view of the world with more scientific knowledge of navigation and geography.

As Prince Henry explored Ceuta and its markets, where he saw traders offering gold and spices from lands across the Sahara Desert, he wondered about that huge continent to the south. Over the next few months he also wondered about how to reopen trade, because as news spread that Ceuta was in Christian hands, ships and caravans stopped arriving from Libya, Mali, and Timbuktu, and Ceuta's markets fell silent.

Henry had to find other ways to open up Africa to trade and exploration. So he set up headquarters at the bleak southern tip of Portugal, where cliffs jut out into the Atlantic. Here, in 1418, from Sagres, he sent out ships to explore Africa's Atlantic coast.

Cape Bojador was 1,600 km (1,000 miles) down that coast, and it was the outer limit of European knowledge. It was an alarming place, where waves appeared to boil over rocky shoals, and chunks of red cliff fell into the sea in a blood-colored spray. Sailors said it was the end of the world.

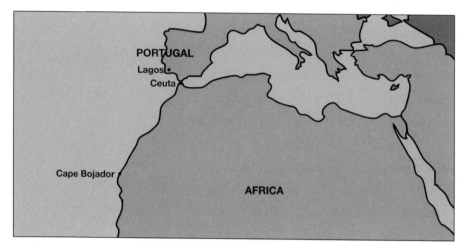

Today's map of Henry the Navigator's world.

But like a child who can't stay away from a locked door, Prince Henry had to know what lay beyond Cape Bojador. Between 1424 and 1434, he sent fifteen expeditions to find out.

Pacing the stone walls of Sagres looking over the Atlantic, Henry waited for news. Over the next decade, his sailors added Madeira and the Azores islands to the Portuguese map of the known world. But he kept pressing them to go beyond Cape Bojador.

This was very un-medieval of him. Most Europeans at the time believed that, as you got closer to the equator, the sea would begin to boil. They thought that Africa was populated by dog-headed people and ants as big as pigs. Medieval Christian faith discouraged investigation of the physical world and told people to concentrate on the afterworld. But a strange transformation had begun in the mind of the Christian prince of Portugal. His curiosity was starting to override his beliefs.

Finally, in 1435, a brave captain named Gil Eannes took a ship beyond Cape Bojador. The sea did not boil. And when sailors went ashore they found not dog-headed people but normal human footprints in the sand.

Henry realized that, to go beyond Cape Bojador, his sailors would

THE MAPMAKER'S BROTHERS

need better boats. So the Christian Prince turned to infidels for help. He ordered ship designers and builders, some of them Arab, to work in secret on a new boat. The caravel proved to be fast and easy to handle; it

THE CARAVEL

The problem with the Portuguese boats was their square-rigged sails – they could sail down the coast of Africa easily enough, but to get back against the wind they had to take huge zigzags. This meant longer voyages – too long for supplies to last. So Sagres ship designers copied the lateen rigging – with triangular sails – from Arab caravos. This enabled the new "caravels" to sail closer to the wind, making the return trip much faster.

Above all, the caravels were easy to handle. A child could do it, and some did. In 1446, the crew of one of Henry's ships was ambushed at the River Gambia in Africa. Africans determined to fight off slave-raiding parties killed more than 20 Portuguese sailors with poisoned arrows. The only people left to sail the ship the 2,400 kilometers (1,500 miles) home were an African lad, two Portuguese cabin boys, and a teenager with some nautical training, named Aires Tinoco, who became the captain.

For two months, always in fear that they would be spotted by Muslim traders, the teenagers sailed onward, keeping the African coast on their right and the Pole Star straight ahead. Finally they saw another ship. To their joy, it was a Spanish corsair, which led them home to Portugal. The young sailors were taken straight to Prince Henry. Their story became one of Portugal's great heroic tales.

permitted the Portuguese to sail farther down the African coast than ever before. Soon the sailors started bringing back captives, first as proof of where they had been, and then as slaves, whose sale helped pay for more voyages.

Prince Henry also needed more information, and that meant more maps. He may have seen the maps of al-Idrisi, or the writings of the pilgrim Ibn Battuta who crossed the Sahara to Mali and Timbuktu. We know that Henry ordered Muslim merchants to visit him at Sagres. He consulted Jewish cartographers from the island of Majorca who had better communications with Muslim traders, pilgrims, and sailors than Christians did.

Majorca's most famous mapmaking family was named Cresques. In 1375, Abraham Cresques produced a set of maps (now known as the *Catalan Atlas*) for the king of Aragon to present to the king of France. The panel showing Africa would have been especially intriguing to someone like Prince Henry: Cresques has painted the King of Mali, a black man dressed as a European king, holding a huge nugget of gold. Prince Henry persuaded Abraham's son, Jafuda Cresques — known as the Master Mapmaker of Majorca — to train a new generation of mapmakers at Sagres.

Henry wasn't the only member of the royal family who was interested in maps. His brother Prince Pedro had spent years traveling, looking at maps in the great courts of Europe. Portuguese rulers had come to realize that maps were important in conquering the world and dominating trade — especially the profitable slave trade. So they passed a royal charter, or law, forbidding anyone to make maps or globes of new African discoveries without official permission. But by the 1430s, Prince Pedro had no more time for researching maps in foreign countries. Matters in Portugal were becoming too complicated.

King Joao died in 1433. At first his sons kept their promise and stuck together. In fact, Duarte, Pedro, Henry, and the youngest, Fernando,

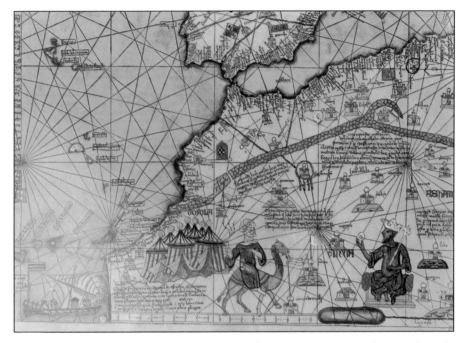

This panel from the Catalan Atlas, *made by Abraham Cresques around 1375, shows the Mediterranean coast, a portion of West Africa, and a camel caravan crossing the Sahara Desert.*

decided to repeat their conquest of Ceuta by capturing the North African Muslim city of Tangier. This time it was a disaster. Three Portuguese assaults were beaten back and Henry's horse was killed right from under him. The enemy forced the Portuguese princes to negotiate a humiliating peace. Until his brothers returned Ceuta, the Muslims would keep Prince Fernando as hostage.

So Duarte, Henry, and Pedro left their brother in enemy hands, and for years, Prince Fernando waited confidently to be freed. Unfortunately, it turned out that Fernando's brothers valued Ceuta too highly. Betraying their promise to their mother, the brothers stalled in order to keep the city they'd won in their glorious youth. Five years of negotiations dragged on while their youngest brother waited in a stinking prison cell. He died of dysentery — fever and diarrhea — in 1443.

THE CATALAN ATLAS

The Catalan Atlas is probably Europe's greatest medieval map. Abraham Cresques (and probably his son Jafuda) hand-painted its brilliant colors and gold leaf onto twelve sheets of sheepskin around 1375.

It's not quite what we think of as an atlas – a collection of maps – because it also includes astrological charts. But much of it is recognizable. The Asian panels name such places as "Delly" (Delhi in India) and "Mecho" (Mecca in Arabia) from information gathered from Arab and Italian travelers. One panel shows the camels of Marco Polo's caravan as it made its way to "Catayo" or Cathay (China).

The mapmakers incorporated scientific elements from the "portulan" (port-finding) charts of Mediterranean sailors. Their map is one of the earliest maps to show a "wind rose" – the circle of points that show where the winds blow from: North, South, East, and West.

By this time, Duarte had died too, leaving the throne to his son Afonso, who was still a child. With no strong ruler, it looked like Portugal would slide back into civil war. The nobles voted to make Pedro the acting king. Like Henry, Pedro was greedy for riches. He started to buy his own maps and send his own caravel boats down the coast of Africa, in direct competition with Henry. Then Pedro was murdered in 1449 by some nobles at Alfarrobeira. Some people whispered that Henry knew about the murder and could have prevented it. Henry certainly failed to protect his brother's wife and children, who fled for their lives. It's also suspicious that it took Henry five years to finally organize an elaborate funeral for Pedro.

Meanwhile, young Afonso became king. Around 1457, he commissioned a great Venetian mapmaker, a priest named Fra Mauro, to work on a *mappamundi*, a map of the world. Afonso's mappamundi has been lost, but another Fra Mauro map survives — one showing Africa as a continent you could sail around. This was just the encouragement Henry needed.

By now Henry was an old man, with memories of a broken promise to his mother and his failure to prevent the deaths of his brothers Pedro and Fernando. If these memories bothered Henry, it didn't show in the single-mindedness with which he kept pushing his sailors to explore more African coastline. By 1457, Henry's sailors had crossed the Tropic of Cancer. Soon after, they reached Cape Verde and that part of Africa where it no longer bulges to the west but starts to curve eastward again.

Showing Henry holding a model of a caravel and looking out to sea, this statue captures the Prince's obsession with exploration and discovery.

When news came back to Sagres that his sailors were now following the African coast eastward, Henry may have hoped that his expeditions would soon reach the fabulous wealth of India. But he never found out that there was much more land to be discovered before India; he fell ill and died on November 13, 1460.

Henry left no children, yet in a sense fathered many lives. He was the first to organize an expert team of discoverers – shipbuilders, navigators, and mapmakers. And he was one of the first to understand that the urge to perfect existing maps would encourage generations of Portuguese explorers who came after him. One was Bartolomeu Dias, who in 1487 sailed a Portuguese ship around the Cape of Good Hope at the tip of Africa. Ten years later, Vasco da Gama reached India. In 1500, Alvares Cabral was blown off course as he tried to follow da Gama's route around Africa; he crossed the south Atlantic to discover Brazil. Then there was the greatest navigator of his age, Ferdinand Magellan, a Portuguese navigator sailing under the flag of the Spanish kingdom of Seville. Magellan died in the Philippines, but his expedition was the first to sail round the world in 1522. All these heroic explorers owed some of their achievements to Henry.

But Henry was also father of Europe's slave trade – tens of millions of human lives wrecked in cruelty and exile. If the ghosts of his brothers haunt Henry's story, so do theirs.

THE MAPMAKER'S BELIEFS

Gerard Mercator

IT IS THE cold spring of 1544, and Gerardus Mercator, father of six children and one of the most famous names in mapmaking, expects that at any moment his dungeon door will be thrown open. Then he will be dragged out and executed – perhaps burned at the stake – because Queen Maria, sister of the Holy Roman Emperor Charles V, has ordered that her holdings in the Low Countries (modern-day Belgium and parts of Holland) be cleansed of people with suspicious religious beliefs.

As the mapmaker stares at the stone walls of his cell in Rupelmonde Castle, he wonders whether his maps will be used as evidence against him. How can the map of a serious, internationally respected scientist reveal his private beliefs? Easily, in the troubled times of Gerard Mercator. It is a time of terrible religious wars and upheavals, a world where the agents of the Emperor try to enforce loyalty to the Catholic Church by scrutinizing any clue – even the shape of a map – for signs of secret loyalty to the new Protestant forms of Christianity, which are seen as treason against the Emperor.

Mercator knows a secret: maps are never purely scientific. Mapmakers select what seems important and leave other things out. Maps always reflect their maker's beliefs.

The very first map Mercator published, in 1537, was of the Holy Land at the time of the Exodus, showing the Israelites' route as they fled slavery in Egypt. Where other mapmakers of the time drew tiny figures of slaves passing through the Sea of Reeds pursued by Pharoah's armies, Mercator had drawn only the Sea's parted waves — as if inviting the readers of his maps to imagine themselves as the Israelites. Inviting ordinary people into the pages of the Holy Bible to interpret it for themselves — that was what Protestantism was about.

And this isn't the only map that casts suspicion on the man in Rupelmonde Castle's freezing dungeon. In his first map of the world, published in 1538, Mercator showed the Earth as if he had split its skin down one side and spread two hemispheres apart like sides of a heart. The heart-shaped projection (map format) is no help to anyone trying to understand the shapes of continents, but it suggests that the world is like the human heart. The Protestant reformer Martin Luther taught that Christians should look into their own hearts to seek God. For a mapmaker to use the world-as-heart design is to play with fire.

Mercator knows all that. But he also knows that his is the great age of geographical discovery, and that never before have the design and making of maps been so exciting.

Gerard Kremer was born in 1512 near the Belgian city of Antwerp. (*Kremer* is Flemish for "merchant"; he later changed it to its Latin version, *Mercator*.) With his parents, traveling shoemakers, he lived in a region of market and university towns. The people they met were buzzing with news of the latest discoveries — Portuguese voyages around Africa, and the voyages of Christopher Columbus and John Cabot across the North Atlantic. Just five years before Mercator's birth, a German monk named Martin Waldseemüller had produced a map of the world labeling the new-found lands "America" and showing them to be a

THE MAPMAKER'S BELIEFS

THE GENIUS OF GEMMA

Finding a way to figure out longitude – that is, how far east or west you were – was a big problem for sailors. Failure to calculate longitude could mean a ship missing a port and a chance to get fresh water; or it might lead the ship to run aground on a rocky coast. In 1533, Gemma Frisius proposed a solution. He pointed out that the world took twenty-four hours to spin around in a circle. If you divided the 360 degrees of that circle into twenty-four parts, you got one hour's difference for each 15 degrees you moved west or east. So if travelers could compare the time at a fixed point (home port or some internationally agreed-upon starting point) with the time at their present position, they would know how far east or west they were.

Gemma had other ideas about mapmaking too. The flat landscape of the Low Countries where he and Gerard Mercator lived was ideal for the development of new surveying techniques. If you climbed a church tower, you could see roads and canals running in straight lines off into the distance. Gemma described how to survey an area of great size using a method called triangulation. A surveyor would walk the distance between two church towers, A and B, very carefully. Next, he would climb tower A and measure the angle between the sightlines to tower B and a third tower C, or angle BAC. He'd do the same at tower B, measuring angle ABC. With this information – the length of a base line and two angles – he could calculate the length of the other two sides of the triangle – the distances AC and BC.

continent. Young Gerard must have figured that mapmaking looked like a more exciting way of making a living than mending shoes.

A rich uncle paid the boy's school fees, and Gerard studied calligraphy. He became very skilled at a newly-invented script that sloped gently to the right, was easy to read, and was called "italic." Gerard also studied engraving and tool-making. And he took mathematics under the brilliant mathematician Gemma Frisius at the University of Louvain.

Gemma was famous, not only for writing books on surveying, but also for designing scientific instruments and globes. Charles V, the Holy Roman Emperor, wanted a Gemma globe so much, he issued royal charters to protect Gemma's copyright so that the scientist could make him a state-of-the-art version. Gemma couldn't do this on his own, so he brought in collaborators, including his promising student. Gerard Mercator was hired to write the globe's place names in his special, elegant italics.

The globe's face was to be printed on twelve flat pieces of paper and then glued in place. As you know if you have ever tried to wrap a round present with a flat piece of wrapping paper, the result is bunching and mess — unless you trim the paper first. Mercator lettered his map onto twelve separate gores, pieces shaped like elongated footballs, to avoid bunching. Working on this project probably made him think harder than ever about how to represent a round world on a flat map.

The Gemma-Mercator globe of 1535 drew on the latest information from explorers. Decorated with sailing ships and tiny drawings of exotic people, it showed Africa's shape and length more precisely than any previous map had done. It also depicted more than fifty-five individual place names in the Americas. But it wasn't that accurate: The Mediterranean looked longer and skinnier (the way the ancient Greek geographer Ptolemy had calculated) than we now know it to be. And the globe featured a huge southern continent, which scientists convinced themselves should exist to keep the planet in balance.

THE MAPMAKER'S BELIEFS

One of Mercator's sources of information for this polar map of the Arctic was a monk who claimed to have gone there and who said that the top of the Earth was like a giant bathtub drain. "The water rushes round and empties into the earth just as if one were pouring it through a filter funnel," Mercator wrote. In the drain's center was a rock, which the mapmaker figured was a giant magnet.

Working on the Gemma globe must have made young Mercator feel that his future was fairly secure. Around this time, he married a girl named Barbara Schelleken. Like her husband, she was interested in new religious beliefs. The two of them would end up paying for this interest.

In nearby Antwerp, around the time that Mercator was finishing his first globe, Catholic Church officials arrested the English theologian and printer John Tyndale. One of Tyndale's crimes was to translate the Bible into English so it could be read by ordinary people, and not just priests. Just a few weeks after Mercator's marriage, Tyndale was executed for heresy. Because printers were the people who published new editions of the Bible, the whole printing profession — engravers, calligraphers, and cartographers as well — came under suspicion.

Barbara and her husband tried to keep their beliefs quiet and concentrate on work and raising their children. By 1540 they had two sons, two daughters, and so much new information about the latest geographical discoveries that the Gemma globe of 1536 needed to be updated. To drum up sales, Mercator wrote that his new, improved model would have the latest information for "Zipangri" (Japan), "the lowest parts of Africa," and details about the American interior.

Emperor Charles V was so pleased with Mercator's globe of 1541 that he commissioned the mapmaker to design a set of surveying and drafting instruments. But the Emperor's patronage did not stop the agents of his sister, Queen Maria, from investigating Mercator. In February 1544, Barbara heard rumors that her husband was to be arrested for suspicious religious beliefs. She told him to slip out of town. She was alone when she answered the door to the men sent by the same church officials who had executed John Tyndale.

Barbara told them that her husband had gone away on innocent family business, to visit his rich uncle. But the officials tracked Mercator to Rupelmonde and arrested him in the street. Now they had two offences to charge him with: heresy and — because he left Louvain — resisting arrest. He was thrown inside the high, grim walls of Rupelmonde Castle.

All through the spring and summer, Barbara pestered powerful friends in the church and at the university to write the Queen and beg for her husband's life. Many sent letters, at great risk to themselves. Meanwhile, Barbara was frightened to learn that more than forty suspected heretics

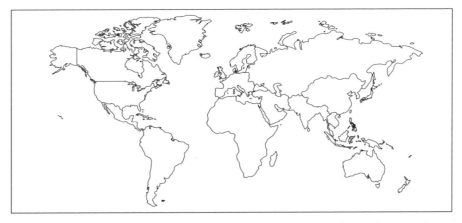

On the Mercator projection shown above, scale and therefore area are distorted more and more towards the extreme north and south. Greenland, for example, is shown to be almost as big as South America. Compare this to the more recent Robinson projection below, which does not exaggerate Greenland and other northern countries so much.

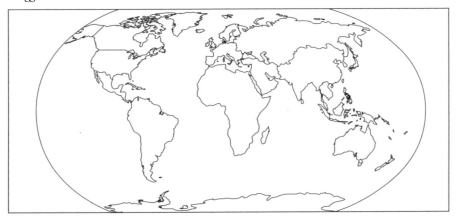

were arrested, tortured, and executed in Louvain and Rupelmonde. But after seven months, Mercator was released from Rupelmonde Castle, and back into his family's arms.

Once you are under suspicion, however, its shadow does not go away. In 1552 the Mercators piled their belongings onto a cart and left Louvain, heading eastward away from Queen Maria's domains. In Duisburg, under the protection of the Dukes of Julich and Cleves, Mercator and his family settled into a new life. The Emperor sent a welcome commission, asking Mercator to make two new small globes. But Mercator's interests now lay in finding ways of drawing the round Earth onto a flat surface.

In 1554, Mercator produced a great map of Europe that used a grid of best estimates of latitude and longitude. This map portrayed the Mediterranean more correctly than before, trimmed down in size (the trouble with maps is that they often force you to correct your notions of what you thought was big and important in the world).

Since his imprisonment, Mercator took care that his maps would not endanger his family. His maps from the 1550s acknowledged the Catholic Church's power, prominently marking the Catholic Church headquarters at the Vatican in Rome. And wherever a small city had a bishop, he made it more prominent than a larger city that had no Catholic leader. The map's subtle message was that the power of the Church trumps political power.

THE MERCATOR PROJECTION

Mercator knew that sailors who depended on their compasses for long ocean crossings had a problem. If you placed a compass on the surface of a globe and then tried to steer a straight line along the compass bearing, you would spiral slowly but inexorably towards one of the poles. On long journeys, sailors had to constantly correct their compass bearings. How could these curving lines be made straight on a map?

Mercator's breakthrough was to make the lines of longitude – which converge toward the poles on a globe – parallel on a flat map by distorting the distances between them. His strategy makes scale, and therefore area, inaccurate, but it preserves shape and direction.

GERARDVS MERCATOR NATVS IVDOCVS HONDIVS NATVS IN

Shown here on the right with Mercator on the left, Hondius honored Mercator among the classical giants of mapmaking.

Yet Mercator could no more abandon science than he could face jail again. In 1569 he brought out the world map for which he is famous, with the projection that bears his name. The Mercator Projection stretches wide the top and bottom of the Earth's round surface in order to make lines of longitude run parallel and to have them meet lines of latitude at right angles in a neat grid.

The Mercator Projection was enough to assure Mercator a reputation as one of the giants of cartography. But there was more. In his seventies and early eighties Mercator worked with his sons on a book of maps. The title was the old man's idea, borrowed from the Greek myth about Atlas, the giant who holds up the sky on his broad shoulders. When the first *Atlas* was published two years after Mercator's death at age eighty-two, it carried affectionate and respectful tributes by many friends — merchants, map collectors, even his competitors. Here's another tribute — until the middle of the 20th century, sailors were still doing most of their calculations using Mercator's projection. Some still do.

THE MAPMAKER'S FAMILY HONOR

The Cassini Family

IN THE YEAR 1682, a group of scientists led by Abbé Jean Picard and Jean-Dominique Cassini assemble at the Royal Observatory in Paris to meet France's King, Louis XIV. The mapmakers look very grand – it is the age of plumed hats and shoulder-length wigs – but they are as nervous as students before a test. They are about to reveal the map they have worked on for more than twelve years – the first complete map of France drawn by triangulation from an accurately placed meridian (line) of longitude measurements, cross-checked on sightings of the stars – to the most powerful monarch France has ever known.

Louis XIV, known as the Sun King, is such a stickler for formality, he makes his courtiers bow to the royal dinner when it passes them on a tray. He takes his own glory and power very seriously. And the mapmakers know their map is about to challenge both.

The Observatory doors are flung open. The courtiers swan in, followed by His Majesty. The scientists sweep off their hats and bow very low, trailing their plumes across the floor. The Sun King walks slowly over to the table on which the new map is laid out beside the old.

His long-nosed face creases into a frown of displeasure, for the new map shows that, compared to the old image of France, His

Majesty's domains do not extend nearly so far into the Atlantic or the Mediterranean. In fact, France appears to have shrunk.

Does the Sun King feel the urge to cry, "Off with their heads"? If so, his need for accurate maps — to build roads and canals to increase trade, and to enrich (and tax) his people — suppresses it. Looking up, His Majesty complains, "Your survey has cost me more territory than a war." Then he orders his royal mapmakers to carry on.

This Jean-Dominique Cassini will do — and so will his son, grandson, and great-grandson, making the Cassinis one of the world's greatest dynasties of mapmaking.

The "corrected Map of France," by the team under Abbé Jean Picard and J-D Cassini, was drawn by Gabriel de La Hire in 1682. It shocked the French by revealing glaring differences between their ideas about France's size and the true outline of their country.

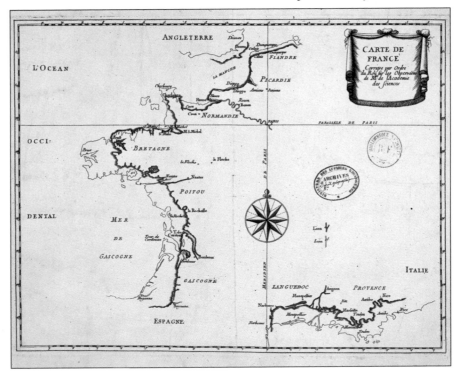

When Giovanni Domenico Cassini first arrived in France in 1668 from his native Italy (where he had been astronomer to the Pope), Europe was a mess — at least in mapmaker's terms. In France, every district, every type of shopkeeper had a different system of measurement. In Paris, an aune — roughly 1 meter (3 feet) — of cotton was shorter than an aune of linen. (Or was it longer? Everyone was confused.) Huge regions of France had never been mapped. Peasants

MAPPING BY THE SKIES

All over the world, since ancient times, sailors and mapmakers have checked their location by consulting the position of heavenly bodies. The sun shines directly down on the equator twice a year. On the longest day of the year in the northern hemisphere it shines directly down on the Tropic of Cancer (that is, a pole in the ground there casts no shadow). On the shortest day in the northern hemisphere, the sun has moved south, and shines directly down over the Tropic of Capricorn. The stars also move with the seasons. Watching the sun and the position of the stars in the night sky enabled people to tell how far north and south they were – that is, latitude.

Astronomy was also important to surveyors. When they set about to survey France, the Cassinis used large quadrants (a quarter of a circle mounted on a pedestal and fitted with a telescope) and sextants (a sixth of a circle) to measure the angle between the horizon and a star, or other heavenly body. By the end of the 18th century, the devices to measure horizontal and vertical angles were combined to form the theodolite.

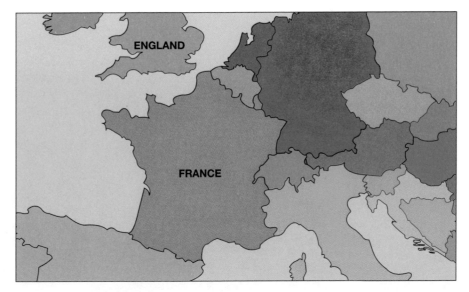

Today's map of the Cassinis' France.

attacked surveyors because they suspected – rightly – that if the extent of their property was formally recorded, they would have to pay more taxes.

At university in Bologna Cassini had studied everything from bugs to blood transfusions, but he was best known for his book about the moons of Jupiter, published in 1668. Cassini's expertise in astronomy made him a real asset in mapmaking. Since Louis XIV was inviting Europe's top scientists to his court, he asked the Pope if he could borrow his astronomer. On arriving in Paris, Giovanni Domenico Cassini was so delighted to find himself among such men as Jean Picard and the great Dutch scientist Christiaan Huygens, he took out French citizenship and changed his name to Jean-Dominique.

In 1669, the Sun King commanded his scientists to correct the existing maps of France, determining its borders east and west from a brass line set into the floor in the middle of the Royal Observatory in Paris. Led at first by Picard, the mapmakers set out to survey a line running north and south between a tower in the town of Malvoisine near Paris

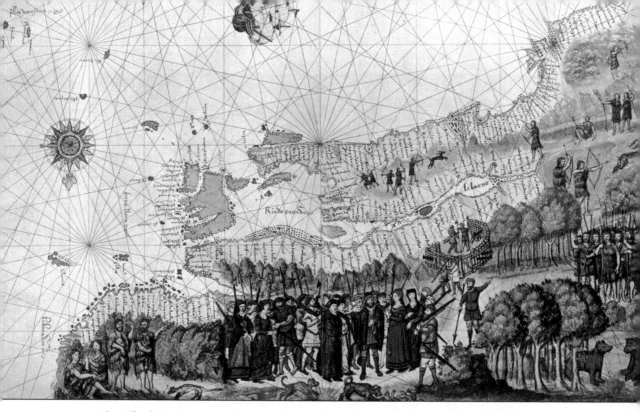

The Vallard Chart of 1547, showing the "Landing of Jacques Cartier" in the New World, is a beautiful thing, but it shows the inaccurate state of French mapmaking before the time of the Cassinis. South is at the top, and the St. Lawrence River flows into a wilderness in which the Great Lakes do not even appear.

and a clock tower in the town of Sourdon near Amiens. The surveyors sent these new measurements back to headquarters in Paris.

Abbé Picard died not long after Louis XIV inspected the first corrected map of France. When Cassini took over the project, he began finding problems with the first survey. A degree of latitude that Picard had measured in the north of France seemed shorter than what Cassini found in the south.

Most people thought the Earth was perfectly round. Cassini proposed that it was not a perfect sphere but was egg-shaped, longer in the middle and shorter at the top. Other scientists, including England's Isaac Newton, insisted the spin of the Earth made it more like a grapefruit, bulgy in the middle and flattened at the Poles. As he grew older and

THE MAPMAKER'S FAMILY HONOR

more respected, Cassini defended his egg theory vigorously. What he was really defending was the accuracy of his first series of observations — in other words, his reputation — and the job that he was planning to pass on to his son Jacques Cassini (known as Cassini II). The debate over Earth's shape became a question of French versus English approaches to the problem, and a matter of national and family honor.

Cassinis I and II decided to run a new survey from Paris to Dunkirk on the English Channel, and from Paris south to the Spanish border. When the old man died at age eighty-seven in 1712, Cassini II took over the family cause, still insisting that the Earth was an egg, and that lines of latitude got shorter as you went north. By the mid-1700s, even Frenchmen were beginning to doubt this. One young mathematician, Pierre-Louis Moreau de Maupertuis, twenty years younger than Jacques Cassini, made it his personal cause to prove that the royal mapmaker was holding France back from cutting-edge science with his stubbornness.

To resolve the dispute, everyone agreed there should be a new round of measurement and mapmaking. In 1735, France's new king, Louis XV, agreed to finance two costly expeditions to determine the shape of the Earth. One, under Charles Marie de la Condamine, set off to Peru to measure the length of a degree of latitude at the equator. The other, led by Maupertuis himself, headed for the Arctic Circle in Finland.

After fifteen months, Maupertuis and his team returned with heroic stories of bone-chilling cold, tales of plagues of summer mosquitoes — and measurements that showed the length of a degree of latitude at the Arctic Circle was longer — by about ½ kilometer (⅓ mile) in today's measurements — than a degree measured in the middle of France. Maupertuis said the Cassinis were wrong.

But Maupertuis had used English instruments to take his measurements, Cassini II pointed out. Surely this must have biased him to accept the English idea about the Earth's shape. In public, Cassini II played the objective scientist. But Maupertuis complained that in private Cassini raised petty objections to the Finland survey, and would not shut up. Maupertuis fought back by publishing anonymous pamphlets insulting the Cassini family's scientific abilities.

Nine years after the second team set out, Condamine and his men straggled back from Peru. They had clambered up the Andes Mountains, contracted fevers in the Amazon jungle, and fought so bitterly with one another that they were no longer on speaking terms. But their measurements also confirmed that the Earth was indeed wider in the middle. Voltaire, the great French intellectual, joked, "The expedition flattened both the poles and the Cassinis."

By this time, Jacques Cassini's son, César-François Cassini (Cassini III), had taken over as royal mapmaker. It was up to him to make peace in 1743 by agreeing that Newton and Maupertuis were right. In any case, there were more important tasks at hand. By the 1740s, the Cassinis had covered France with 400 separate triangulations. No country in the world had ever before been so thoroughly measured.

But many French people hated the whole project. Peasants often tried to steal the surveyors' equipment. In the 1760s, in one remote mountain town, villagers pulled a surveyor from his ladder and attacked him with their hay-cutting tools. When they finally let the poor man go, he was streaming with blood. The villagers told a local magistrate investigating the attack that the surveyor was "a sorcerer who had come to harm them . . . and to increase the income tax . . . ."

Another danger was that the king might lose interest in the mapping project. He did. Royal funding was cut in 1756. So Cassini III rounded up private investors and turned his mapmaking into a profitable business, selling charts to the public. He also invited English surveyors to compete with the French in measuring latitude and longitude around the English Channel — mapping was beginning to transcend national boundaries.

THE MAPMAKER'S FAMILY HONOR

THE METRIC SYSTEM

Before the French Revolution, measurements were so chaotic that France's scientists and shopkeepers alike were clamoring for reform. In 1790 the National Assembly ordered the French Academy of Sciences to come up with "an invariable standard" – some unit derived from nature, around which could be built a system in divisions and multiples of ten. But how long would the new unit, to be called a meter from the Greek word for measurement, be? The Academy decided it would be one ten-millionth of the distance between the North Pole and the equator. In 1791, under the direction of Cassini IV, two scientists set out to do yet another triangulation of France, to determine that total distance – and then one ten-millionth of it.

The two – Jean Delambre and Pierre Méchain – worked for seven years. The old government was overthrown in the French Revolution, their boss Cassini was imprisoned, and the new regime threatened to call off the entire project. Mobs threw them in jail. They got sick. Worst of all, Méchain fell into a depression and disappeared. When finally tracked down by his long-suffering wife, he said he couldn't finish the job properly. So Delambre and Madame Méchain did the final calculations. Somehow the meter was defined and, in 1799, was cast in a rod of pure platinum.

In the 20th century, calculations based on satellite readings of the distance from the North Pole to the equator revealed that the 1799 meter is imperfect – it's about 0.2 mm (1/140 inch) short. Now the meter is redefined as the distance light travels in a vacuum in 1/299,792,458 of a second. Today 95 percent of countries use the metric system (the U.S. and Liberia are among the holdouts that do not).

Cassini III, the peacemaker, died of smallpox in 1784, and his son Cassini IV (named Jean-Dominique, just like his great-grandfather) became director of France's Royal Observatory. He was made head of the project to develop the measurement of a single perfect meter, which would form the basis of the new metric system. And he published the Carte de Cassini in 1789.

The Carte de Cassini is drawn to a scale of 1:86,400 and is printed on 184 sheets. Each sheet, folded and delicate, is so detailed, you can see tiny church steeples and windmills. When the maps showing Paris were published for the public in 1793, they became bestsellers.

But 1793 was also a year of revolution. The king lost his head on the guillotine. So did his top scientists, many who were friends of the Cassini family. Mobs searched the Royal Observatory where Cassini IV lived, and terrorized his family. Cassini IV dismissed the mobs as "Don Quixotes," or crazy dreamers. He did not realize how much France's poor blamed their miserable lives and heavy taxes on the king and his mapmakers.

Some of the young researchers who worked for Cassini IV at the Observatory did know, however. Alexandre Ruelle had been hired by Cassini IV to work as a guard at the Observatory and to take basic sightings of stars and planets. Astronomical observation is a difficult job calling for a lot of patience, and Ruelle wasn't very good at it. Cassini IV was probably tough on the young researcher; after all, this Cassini was the fourth generation of the family that had mapped France. In any case, Ruelle hated his boss. One night, he overheard a fellow guardsman come home drunk, yelling, "Cassini the aristocrat must die!" This gave Ruelle an idea.

Ever since the king's execution, revolutionary tribunals were running France. Ruelle went to one and declared that Cassini IV was an old-style aristocrat who exploited his researchers and stole their hard work. The tribunal took the complaints seriously. The members decided to make Cassini pay for his family's connections to the dead king. First they fired him as director of the Royal Observatory. Then they seized his maps of

Giovanni Domenico Cassini is shown in this engraving from 1712 with a telescope in the background, to signify that he was not only a major mapmaker, but also an astronomer who discovered four moons of the planet Saturn. The founder of the Cassini dynasty that mapped France for four generations, he is known as Cassini I.

France, the project for which his family had been responsible for more than a century. When Cassini IV protested, he was thrown in prison.

But Ruelle wanted more — the boss's head. So he pestered the tribunal to bring Cassini IV to trial and the guillotine. At last, others at the Observatory stood up for their master. They told the tribunal that Ruelle was a poor scientist. They said he had made a major error in an observation of the sun and was trying to frame Cassini. Now it was Ruelle's turn to be thrown in jail.

Cassini IV was lucky. He spent just seven months behind bars, expecting each day to be marched up the guillotine's wooden stairs and forced to lay his head under its knife. Instead, he was finally set free. But he was still disillusioned, so he left Paris and moved to the country. In a letter to a friend, he wrote that mapmaking and star-watching meant nothing to him any more. The greatest scientists of his age had been killed by the mob, he said, but what saddened him even more was that he had seen scientists "themselves up in arms, divided against one another."

It was too much. Cassini IV convinced his son that the great mapmaking dynasty should end. There would never be a Cassini V. The son of Cassini IV became a botanist.

THE MAPMAKER'S HANDS

Captain James Cook

THE HORRIFIED MEN and cabin boys of His Majesty's ships the Resolution and the Discovery, anchored in Hawaii's Kealakekua Bay, peer into the basket. They see a pair of severed human hands. They know at once whose hands they are.

Large, brown, and callused from years at sea, the hands have a purplish scar running around the right thumb. The men know that these hands have ordered men whipped, but have also fine-tuned scientific instruments of delicate precision. They have written journals in a confident, sloping script that looks as orderly as a fleet of ships leaning before a steady wind. They have drawn some of the most accurate maps the world has ever seen. The British sailors would know those hands anywhere. They have been chopped from the body of their captain, the legendary James Cook.

James Cook was born on October 27, 1728, to a poor Scottish farmworker's family in the north of England. Tall and intelligent, the boy had a magnetic ability to attract attention from people who were willing to help him on his way. He also had a boundless appetite for adventure, and wrote in his journal, "I want to go as far as I think possible for man to go."

So he went to sea — to the merchant fleet that sailed out of the town of Whitby, hauling coal down the English coast in flat-bottomed boats of the sort known as Whitby cats. But he turned down the chance to become captain of his own cargo ship. He started from the bottom again as an able seaman in the Royal Navy.

In 1758, the ambitious young man was shipped to Canada to fight the French. On his first Atlantic crossing, twenty-six of his crewmates perished from scurvy, a fatal vitamin deficiency. Those who survived spent the winter in Halifax. Unlike his fellow sailors, who mostly drank and fought, Cook spent his time before the final assault on Quebec City learning how to make maps from surveyor Samuel Holland.

To stop the English from sailing up the St. Lawrence River to attack them, the French had removed all the buoys and markers warning sailors of shallow or dangerous waters. All winter, Holland and Cook surveyed the St. Lawrence, taking soundings of the river's depths and making notes ("good Anchoring here in Soft Clay Ground"). Thanks to their

In this beautiful setting, Hawaii's Kealakekua Bay, Captain James Cook was killed on February 14, 1779. A small monument has been erected to honor Cook's memory, and the fact that he mapped the Pacific almost from pole to pole.

charts, when the British fleet sailed upriver in the spring of 1759, not one ship ran aground.

After General Wolfe and the British defeated the French outside Quebec City on the Plains of Abraham, Cook sailed home to London. He was thirty-three, and unemployed. But he must have been sure of himself, for he proposed marriage to Miss Elizabeth Batts, a pretty London shop girl. A week after their wedding, in late December 1762, Cook strode into the British Admiralty for new orders.

His way had been smoothed by letters from his commanding officers in Canada that spoke of "Mr. Cook's capacity and genius." Impressed, the Royal Navy's admirals made him Master Surveyor and told him to chart the wild 9,600-kilometer (6,000-mile) coast of Newfoundland.

The usual method of surveying a coast at that time was called a running traverse, and involved triangulating headlands and high points of land from the pitching deck of a moving ship. Master Surveyor Cook decided to combine the running traverse with time-consuming but more accurate surveys from land. Everyday he had to row ashore, measure a base line, fix flags at the end points, and then sight the angles from those points to a third position. The results were so good, his charts were still in use a hundred years later.

Cook's new career nearly ended August 6, 1764, when a powder horn blew up, almost taking his right thumb off. A good surgeon stitched him up – but for the rest of his life, Cook's hand was scarred from thumb to wrist.

Cook spent three years on the Newfoundland survey, his reputation growing with each shipment of beautiful new charts sent home. So the Royal Navy promoted him again. In 1768, he was given his own ship and told to sail to Tahiti in the Pacific to watch the planet Venus cross the sun. There he was to open a secret envelope with further orders from the Royal Navy.

Why send a costly expedition to watch stars? England desperately wanted to make a major scientific discovery to compete with the French, the master mapmakers of the age. Besides, the French, Dutch, and Spanish were already claiming Pacific lands, and the English wanted a share of the action and the profits. They also wanted to solve the mystery of the great southern continent, the one whose existence was predicted by

PACIFIC ISLANDS MAPS

When Europeans began to explore the far-flung islands of the vast Pacific, they probably didn't realize that the local people there were among the most remarkable sailors the world has ever seen. These islanders had sailed with their families and their livestock, in open rafts, across the world's largest ocean. Hopping from island to island, they had established trade routes and started colonies.

Of course, the Pacific Islanders made maps. Few survive, but there is a rare example in the Maritime Museum in Greenwich, London, made by inhabitants of the Marshall Islands in the 19th century. (Marshall Islanders guarded the information by which they made these maps as state secrets.) The Marshall Islands map is a rectangular frame of palm fibers. Thinner fibers curve across the frame, representing the direction of ocean currents. Small seashells lashed at key places on the curving fibers represent islands. Marshall Islands sailors could orient the frame according to the direction of the waves, and, by watching the currents, sail long distances to remote islands.

Ptolemy, Mercator, and other geographers. The reliable Cook was just the man to discover it. "The world," wrote Cook, "will hardly admit of an excuse for a man leaving a coast unexplored he has once discovered."

At Cook's request, the Navy agreed to let him sail a Whitby cat. Cook patrolled the shipyards to make sure that the remodeling of his cat, the Endeavour, would make her ship-shape. He had the ship loaded with strange cargo: supplies of sauerkraut and carrot marmalade. Cook wanted to prevent scurvy, and he suspected (correctly) that if he fed his sailors – he referred to them as the People – a better diet than the Navy's traditional salt beef, he could save their lives. The People were told that if they didn't eat their vegetables, they would be whipped.

Off they sailed to South America. In January 1769, the ship reached Cape Horn at the southern tip, a place where the Atlantic and the Pacific collide in horrendous storms. But Cook seemed able to handle anything the ocean threw in his face. He was strict, but the People had to admit that Cook's sailing skills were superb.

When the Endeavour dropped anchor in lush, green Tahiti, the People went crazy, chasing local women and gorging on roast pig. Meanwhile Cook set up an observatory and successfully recorded the transit of Venus. Then he opened the envelope with his secret orders: Find the Great Southern Continent – or prove that it does not exist.

Cook ordered the Endeavour to set sail straight for the South Pole. Finding nothing as far south as the 40th latitude but rolling sea, Cook turned the Endeavour west to New Zealand. Its outline was still unmapped – could it be part of the Great Southern Continent?

When the English sailors went ashore and visited abandoned camps of the local people, the Maori, they noticed human bones in cooking pots. A few friendly Maori explained that they didn't eat everybody, just enemies killed in battle. Still, Cook realized that it was too dangerous to survey from land as he had in Newfoundland. He made most of his charts by running traverse.

THE MAPMAKER'S HANDS

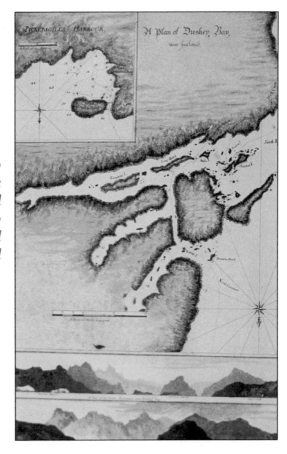

This is Cook's map of Dusky Bay, New Zealand. He declared it to be "one of the most beautiful places which nature unassisted by art could produce." He arrived here first in 1769, and returned again in 1773.

After Cook proved to his own satisfaction that New Zealand was not part of the mysterious southern continent, he set sail for Australia. It had been sighted by Dutch explorer Abel Tasman in 1642, but no European had ever visited Australia's eastern coast. Cook charted 3,200 kilometers (2,000 miles) of it in four months.

Then he discovered Australia's Great Barrier Reef by running into it. On August 17, 1770, the Endeavour's hull was pierced and she began to take on water. The shore was far away, and most of the People (including Cook) couldn't swim. They had to pump the Endeavour's leaking hold, or die. Yet even in the crisis, Cook ordered a few men off the pumps to take measurements of longitude — which later proved

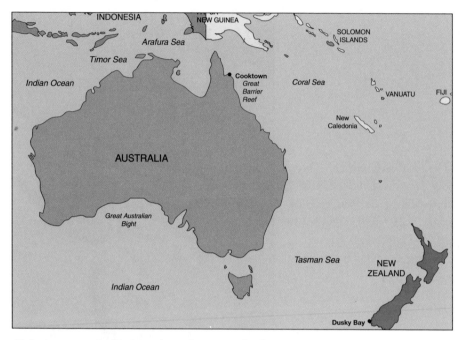

Today's map of Cook's Australia and New Zealand.

admirably accurate. The People patched the leaks by stuffing them with old sails, and threw heavy equipment overboard to lighten the ship. After anxious hours, the tide turned, and the Endeavour floated up and off the reef. The People repaired her and sailed on.

When a tattered but triumphant Endeavour finally returned to England in 1771, Cook should have become famous. His men boasted that he had saved them from scurvy, storms, reefs, and cannibals. When he had set sail, almost a third of the world – the Pacific – was missing from the world map. Now the map was filling in.

Instead of hailing Cook as a hero, London society was more impressed with the ship's botanist, a rich aristocrat named Joseph Banks. Newspapers spoke of "the Banks voyage," and Banks, a snappier writer than Cook, rushed into print with a book about narrow escapes and natural marvels.

But the Admiralty lords knew who the real hero was. They made

THE MAPMAKER'S HANDS

Cook a captain and announced that he would lead a second great voyage of science and discovery. A pair of German botanists, Johann Forster and his son Georg, would replace the grandstanding Banks.

The Admiralty told Cook that his new expedition would carry a device that would solve the riddle of how to calculate longitude – Larcum Kendall's copy of John Harrison's longitude watch – which would let him compare the time at the ship's position with the time back in London. Soon after the voyage began, Cook wrote in his journal, "Our error can never be great, so long as we have so good a guide as the watch."

Aboard the Resolution, Cook kept everything ticking nicely. His People munched their way through the expedition's 9,000 kilograms (20,000 pounds) of "Sour Krout," 135 liters (30 gallons) of carrot marmalade, and 1,000 bunches of raw onions. But Tobias Furneaux, captain of the Resolution's sister ship the Adventure, seemed to think that a bad diet was British navy tradition. After only three months at sea, when the two ships dropped anchor at Cape Town, South Africa, Furneaux had lost several men to scurvy. Cook, who had lost no one, was furious.

In November the two ships sailed south in search of the Great Southern Continent. On a calm January day, the Adventure and the Resolution crossed the Antarctic Circle. Then ice floes began to close in, threatening to crumple the little wooden ships like paper. Cook didn't know that they were just 120 kilometers (75 miles) from the Antarctic coast when they headed back towards open seas.

Fog closed in and separated the Adventure and the Resolution, so each headed to New Zealand for a rendezvous. Captain Furneaux arrived first. Afraid of what Cook would do if his men got scurvy again, he sent a party of ten ashore at Grass Cove to gather wild vegetables. They never returned. A search party the next day found a Maori campsite and parts of the missing crewmates, roasted. Sick at heart, Furneaux set sail for England.

Meanwhile, Cook and the Resolution once again crossed the Antarctic

THE LONGITUDE PRIZE

In 1728, the year James Cook was born, John Harrison entered the contest to win the British government's Longitude Prize of £20,000. Harrison was a carpenter and self-taught watchmaker, and he thought he could design a watch so perfectly balanced and buttressed from shock that it would tell accurate time despite wild waves and extremes of temperature. It would have to be really accurate – if it was out by one minute, a ship's course would be off by 20 kilometers (12.5 miles). The Longitude Board wasn't impressed by Harrison, a poor man with a northern accent. But ever since 1707, when Admiral Sir Clowdisley Shovell had miscalculated longitude and driven four ships onto the rocks off England's south coast, causing the deaths of 2,000 men, the British were willing to consider anything.

Harrison worked on his watch for decades. Finally he produced a shiny watch about the size of a small plate. Its jeweled mechanism was made of special combinations of metals that expanded at different rates – so the watch kept steady time despite extremes of heat and cold – and balances – so the watch would keep ticking even in the worst of gales. Harrison's watch kept almost perfect time on two voyages to the West Indies. However, the aristocrats on the Longitude Board were reluctant to give such a huge amount of money to a lower-class senior citizen, and insisted that a replica of Harrison's watch be submitted to a third test on Captain Cook's second voyage. The copy worked beautifully, and Harrison was finally awarded the Longitude Prize in 1773, when he was seventy-eight years old. Cook liked his copy of the watch so much, he took it on his third voyage too.

Circle – something no one else would do until the next century. They sailed so close to some of the icebergs that the men on deck had to push the ship away with long poles. But there was no sign of land, only great cloud banks above a dazzling whiteness along the horizon, and ice all around.

In 1775 Cook and the Resolution headed home. The People had been gone for three years and seventeen days. They had sailed 110,000 kilometers (70,000 miles), the equivalent of three times round the world. Cook was once again hailed as a hero by his men. They boasted that they would follow him anywhere – which is what they had done.

This time, Cook didn't make the mistake of letting anyone else write about the voyage. This time, he concentrated on getting his journals ready for publication, and taking Mrs. Cook, pregnant with their sixth child, to parties in London's high society before his next mission. For Cook was to search for a route from the Pacific to the Atlantic across the top of North America – the fabled Northwest Passage.

This time, Cook was too busy to visit the shipyards – too busy to stop the shipbuilders from cutting corners and using rotten wood. Cook's inattention to detail would be fatal. On July 12, 1776, the Resolution and her new sister ship, the Discovery, sailed from England.

This time, Cook seemed a changed man. The People were dismayed to see their once sensible captain order men to be flogged for refusing to eat new foods. He always seemed to be angry at himself, as frequent stops to repair his leaky rotten ships reminded him of his failure to prepare properly for the voyage.

But if he was no longer the fair, reliable captain of earlier voyages, he was still skilled, brave, and lucky. Early in 1777, as they crossed the Pacific, intending to chart the west coast of North America, Cook's men sighted a chain of stunning islands. The islanders were so astonished, it was clear that the English were the first Europeans to arrive there. Cook marked the place with the aid of his longitude watch at around 21 degrees north, 157 degrees west.

Then the ships turned east to North America. Over most of 1778 they sailed from what is now Oregon to Alaska, past some 8,000 kilometers (5,000 miles) of rugged coast, searching for the western end of the Northwest Passage. Cook sailed recklessly in these uncharted lands, reaching almost as close to the North Pole as he had come to the South.

He would never know that, when approaching winter forced the ships to turn back in the Bering Strait, they were just 120 kilometers (75 miles) short of the eastward route they were seeking. The ships headed back to the beautiful islands for rest and repair, and anchored at one the local people called Owhyee — we spell it Hawaii.

The stunning horseshoe-shaped bay where the exhausted sailors dropped anchor is called Kealakekua, or "Path of the Gods." It was the place where Hawaiian legend said that Orono, the god of abundance, would one day arrive in a white-sailed canoe. When two ships sailed into view not only at the appointed place, but at the appointed time of year — harvest time — the astonished Hawaiians went mad with joy. Thousands paddled out to greet the visitors and their tall leader, who was surely Orono himself.

Cook had no idea that the Hawaiians thought he was a god. He only knew that he and his tired men were being given an amazing welcome, and that the natives had draped a magnificent red-feather cloak across his broad shoulders. The English stayed three wonderful weeks, feasting every day.

But the Hawaiians were puzzled by Orono's visit. He was supposed to be the god of abundance, but he and his people were taking more than they gave. Worse, the People chased women, got drunk, and fought. The Hawaiians were happy to see them go.

After a few days at sea, the Resolution's rotten mast broke. The Hawaiians were dismayed when the visitors came back. The Orono legend had said nothing about this. Cook explained courteously that his ships needed more repairs. The Hawaiians shrugged and kept to themselves — except for one, who demanded proof that Cook was a great warrior. Obligingly, Cook showed the scar on his right hand.

Then came the morning of Valentine's Day, February 14. Some young Hawaiians had taken a landing boat from the Discovery the night before. In the morning, Cook and twenty men went ashore to demand its return. The Hawaiians said they didn't have it. The English tried to take an old chief hostage until the boat was given back. But as they started to drag him away, the old chief stumbled. The Hawaiians felt humiliated. They decided they'd had enough. The killing began.

From the decks of the Resolution and Discovery, the sailors could see their fellow sailors being clubbed and speared. And they could see the

The death of Captain Cook is pictured in A Collection of Voyages Round the World, *published in London in 1790. Cook is shown at front left, hand lifted as if to stop the bloodshed to come. In fact, the British boats were much further from shore when Cook died.*

tall figure of their captain — soon the only white face among the brown crowds in Kealakekua Bay. Alone, Captain Cook walked slowly and deliberately, as if willing everyone around him to calm down. One Hawaiian finally decided that even the powerful Cook-Orono was merely human.

The warrior raised his club and bashed the Englishman on the head. Cook staggered and fell on one knee. Another Hawaiian stabbed him in the back of the neck, and he pitched into the shallow water. His men could see him struggling to raise himself onto the shore. After a third crushing club-blow, Cook sank for the last time.

"Thus ended the life of the greatest navigator this or any other nation could boast," wrote Second Lieutenant John Rickman in the ship's log. Aboard the ship, one of the sailors reported something strange — the captain's longitude watch stopped ticking.

Over the next few days, tensions between the Hawaiians and the English stayed high, and more shots were fired. But two brave Hawaiians took their lives in their hands and swam out to the English ships to sing a song of lamentation for Orono. And when the English went ashore for fresh water, they found some of Cook's belongings left for them to take back — including a basket containing their fallen Captain's hands.

When the news reached England, the nation mourned. The King himself was said to be deeply saddened. Cook's old rival, Joseph Banks, wrote a glowing tribute for the London newspapers. Mrs. Cook burned all her husband's love letters. But amid the grief there were also cheers. For a farm laborer's son had gone farther than any man, and he had drawn a mapmaker's lines around the last unknown third of the world.

8

THE MAPMAKER'S NOSE

Alexander von Humboldt

A GIANT IN South America's Andes mountain range, Mount Chimborazo thrusts its great volcanic peak 6,310 meters (21,000 feet) into the clouds. In the year 1802, it is believed to be the world's highest mountain, which is why a small group of men – a young German aristocrat named Alexander von Humboldt, a French botanist named Aimé Bonpland, and several South American guides – are climbing slowly up its slopes.

Chimborazo's first 2,000 meters (6,000 feet) are no problem. Then the team crosses the snow line. The guides turn back, leaving just Humboldt, Bonpland, and a young man named Carlos. As the three trudge upward, the path dwindles to a ridge at times no more than 25 centimeters (10 inches) wide. Sometimes, when the three look over the side, they see cliffs falling away to distant valleys; sometimes there's only blank cloud below.

The air gets thinner and colder, and hail pelts the climbers. Each breath Humboldt takes makes his lungs ache horribly. But his intense curiosity wins out over the pain, and he makes notes on how the vegetation varies as the altitude changes. He also puzzles over the fact that, so near the equator, they are surrounded by snow.

By 5,000 meters (17,000 feet), all three climbers are nauseous, with throbbing headaches. Their noses stream blood. Blood vessels in their eyes have burst, partially blinding them. Blind, sick, and cold, they have to stop. They take out their barometers to measure atmospheric pressure. The mercury stands at 2/1100 inches, by which they calculate that they are at 5,878 meters (19,286 feet). It's not Chimborazo's peak — but it is a world record. Their curiosity at least partially satisfied, the three climbers wipe their bleeding noses and begin to grope their way back down.

Alexander von Humboldt, born in Berlin in 1769, was raised to sniff out challenges and mysteries. His father, a Prussian baron, and his mother, a French Protestant aristocrat, sent Alexander to the University of Göttingen. There he studied with Georg Forster, one of the botanists who had sailed on James Cook's second great voyage. The two men went on hiking trips, Humboldt listening avidly to Forster's tales of the botanical wonderlands of the Pacific. "I can never mention my teacher and friend without feeling the most heartfelt gratitude," Humboldt wrote.

Humboldt wanted to become a botanist like his beloved teacher, but the Baroness von Humboldt had other plans. Her son would have a career in the civil service. So Humboldt studied geology, and at age twenty-three was made Director of Mines in the Prussian state of Franconia. A gung-ho young man, his version of doing his job included scaling cliffs, going down mines, and studying the weird plants he found growing in the gloom.

In 1796, the baroness died, leaving Alexander a small fortune. He quit his job to become what he had always wanted to be: a traveler and scientist. First he bought state-of-the art equipment, including a tiny latitude-measuring instrument for observing the angles of stars —"my snuffbox sextant," he called it. Then he joined up with a French naturalist, the

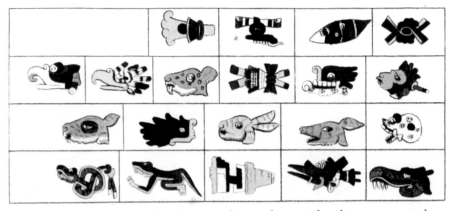

Humboldt took notes on everything he saw in his travels, from plant life to ancient civiliza- tions. He found these hieroglyphs that stand for the days in the Mexican almanac, and put them in his book Researches Concerning the Institutions and Monuments of the Ancient Inhabitants of America, *published in 1814.*

moody, gentle Aimé Bonpland, and the two decided to explore South America.

They applied to join a French expedition. But it was 1798, and the Revolutionary French government, which had so recently guillotined France's top scientists, canceled the expedition in order to prepare for war with England. The two explorers were told that they could not leave Europe because the English were blockading the French coast.

Bonpland and Humboldt refused to be blockaded. They thought they might be able to sail from Spain, so they walked to Madrid – with Humboldt taking altitude measurements the whole way for practice. The King of Spain, intrigued by the intrepid pair, gave them special passports affixed with the royal seal. Finally, in June 1799, they boarded a Spanish mail ship bound for Venezuela and sneaked past the British.

Once there, Humboldt and Bonpland decided to head up the Orinoco River. Two hundred years before, the British privateer Sir Walter Raleigh had drawn charts suggesting that the Orinoco joined the mighty Amazon. Humboldt and Bonpland decided to confirm this. The

Today's map of Humboldt's South America.

fact that the few explorers who ever came back from these jungles told harrowing stories of fevers, hunger, the world's deadliest snakes, and natives who shot poisoned arrows from behind the trees didn't stop them.

Off they went, with Native guides and a guard dog, into 2,775 km (1,725 miles) of agony. Clouds of mosquitoes stung their faces and got into their nostrils. Alligators attacked – ever curious, Humboldt paused to dissect one. They met man-eating fish and leaf-cutting ants that could chomp a road through the forest. Everyone, including the guides, got sick – except the hardy Humboldt, who happily went on collecting rock and plant specimens.

One day the explorers saw a huge horse wade into the river, buckle at the knees, faint, and drown. The guides pointed and cried, "Trembladores!"

Humboldt paid the guides to catch the creatures that killed the horse: electric eels 2 meters (6 feet) long. Moving closer, Humboldt accidentally stepped on one. A massive current shot him a violent jolt of pure pain. As soon as he could grip a pen again, the intrepid scientist wrote, "I do not remember a more dreadful shock!"

THE MAPMAKER'S NOSE

MEASURING ALTITUDE

How do you measure the height of a mountain? Surveyors used barometers to measure changes in atmospheric pressure – the higher you go, the less air pressure there is. The trouble was, early barometers were bulky and fragile. They also used thermometers – the higher up you go, the lower the temperature at which water boils, so you can calculate altitude by taking the temperature of boiling water. The trouble with both methods was that you had to go up the mountain to get a reading of its height.

It was easier to use triangulation of vertical angles. And for that, surveyors used a theodolite, a telescope mounted on special bases so that it could pivot horizontally around a ring marking the angles of the flat plane, and vertically around another ring marking the angle of elevation. With a theodolite, you could take sightings of the mountain's peak from two different positions on the ground and then do your calculations. In 1850, Radhanath Sickdhar, a mathematical genius who worked with the Great Indian Survey, used triangulation to determine that Mount Everest in the Himalayas was in fact the world's highest mountain. Its height of 8,848 meters (29,028 feet) was confirmed by a later Indian survey in 1952.

As Humboldt and Bonpland pressed on, their food ran out and they had to live on wild bananas. Jaguars killed the expedition dog. Yet despite the heat and hideous conditions, they took such accurate readings that Humboldt was later able to produce the first reliable maps of the region. They proved that that a small river, the Casiquiare, links the Orinoco to the Amazon River system.

Mount Chimborazo, an Ecuadorian volcano, was depicted by Humboldt as a cross section, so he could relate the different types of plants he noted to the height at which they grew.

When they finally emerged from the jungle, Humboldt and Bonpland shipped thousands of specimens back to Europe and set off again – west to Ecuador and the Andes Mountains. Here, it was believed, was the world's tallest mountain, Chimborazo. The climb was an ordeal, but they survived it, and Humboldt started setting down the information he had gathered there.

For Humboldt, it was not enough to use maps to show position and place. He was one of the first mapmakers to develop thematic maps, maps that present information in terms of position and patterns: distribution of plants, location of ancient cities, agriculture, water temperature, or storms.

Leaving the Andes, the two scientists mounted their mules and headed for Lima, capital of Peru. There, they hoped to observe the transit of the planet Mercury across the sun and to see the world's greatest ocean.

As they clopped along, they expected to see a vast blue Pacific. Instead, what they saw was gray water under low clouds. Across the sea blew a steady southerly wind, damp and cool in their faces. It always seemed as if it was about to rain, yet local people told them that sometimes it didn't rain for years. In fact, the landscape through which they rode was one of the world's driest deserts. Riding into the ruins of the ancient city of Chanchan, capital of the long-vanished Chimu people, the men were puzzled to see that it had once been a town of reservoirs and gardens. Now the reservoirs were empty, the gardens bone dry.

While Bonpland complained that there were no plants for him to study, Humboldt waded out into the Pacific. Taking the water's temperature, he had a surprise. While the air was hot, the seawater was cool. And there seemed to be a current pushing this cool water northward. Could it be coming all the way from the icy Antarctic?

As the two men rode towards Lima they encountered a smell that nearly gagged them. Fishermen told them the stench was coming from

Modern weather maps like this one are based on the work pioneered by Alexander von Humboldt, who drew lines connecting all the points with a common temperature (isotherms). Once people could see where warm and cool air masses were, they could predict where they would move to.

an island offshore covered in bird droppings. And indeed, the sky over the Pacific was alive with sea birds, wheeling and diving above the waves. Bird droppings, or guano, make splendid fertilizer. Suddenly the two naturalists understood how those ancient cities had sustained themselves in this desert – with guano fertilizer and water brought down from the misty Andes.

But why were there so many birds? Watching them swoop up from the sea with fish flapping in their beaks, Humboldt realized that the strong, cool current supported one of the world's richest marine envi-

ISOLINEAR MAPS

Isolines are lines connecting points of similar information. Places where people prefer tea over coffee, for example, might produce a line between England and China – which would be very useful for anyone selling tea.

The first time isolines appear on a map is in 1686, when British astronomer Sir Edmond Halley (after whom Halley's Comet is named) drew lines connecting points with similar compass readings to produce the first map of magnetic force fields. In 1791 a French mapmaker, J. Dupain-Triel, used isolines to connect similar levels of land above sea level, and made a topographical map. Alexander von Humboldt used isolines on maps he made after his trip to South America, connecting points where the temperature was the same. Because they join points of the same temperature, Humboldt's isolines are really isotherms. In fact, he made the first isothermic map, better known as a weather map.

ronments. But the difference in temperature between the water and the air had a strange effect on Peru's climate. As the sea winds blew over the hot dry land, the air masses warmed up. This increased their capacity to absorb moisture and so, instead of dropping moisture, they sucked up more as they continued inland. The boundaries between warm and cold, between wet and dry — they created life and destroyed it. Humboldt decided to map his discovery.

In 1804, the two naturalists sailed for home, carrying thirty packing cases of some 60,000 species of plants, birds, and beasts. In Europe they were hailed as scientific giants. Bonpland was made head of the botanical gardens in Paris, but eventually returned to South America. As for Humboldt, he spent his family fortune on other expeditions, and on writing and publishing thirty-three books. His unfinished, five-volume *Kosmos* was one of the best-selling books of the 19th century. Humboldt also produced 1,426 maps, including new thematic maps of ancient civilizations, crops, and weather.

Humboldt was a proud man. But he was never comfortable when people called that cold Peruvian current that teemed with life the Humboldt Current; he preferred it to be called the Peru Current. Still, traces of his name are scattered across the Americas: Humboldt mountains, Humboldt counties, and at least eight towns named in his honor. But Humboldt, who lived to be almost ninety, always said that climbing Mount Chimborazo was the greatest honor of all. "Of all mortals," he gloated genially in his old age, "I was the one who had risen highest in the world."

9

THE MAPMAKERS' SENSE OF THE LAND

Mapping North America

AS THE WINTER of 1804 closes in over the Dakota plains, the temperature drops to more than 40° below freezing. Captains Meriwether Lewis and William Clark, and their team — the Corps of Discovery — decide to pass the coldest months in the snug, earth-covered lodges of the Mandan people on the banks of the upper Missouri River.

The Mandan share their lodges with horses and dogs, and even occasional white visitors. In 1798, a Canadian fur-trader and explorer named David Thompson had wintered with them. Now, six years later, it is Lewis and Clark, wrapped in thick bison robes, who sit along with their men around the Mandan campfires.

Just as Thompson had, the Americans question the Mandan about the lands to the west. They examine maps painted on bison hides, and ask the Mandan to draw more maps. Sometimes their hosts use pointed sticks in the campfire ashes. Sometimes they borrow Clark's pen (he is friendlier than Lewis, who seems remote and moody) and sketch great branching rivers on scraps of paper.

The Mandan don't realize who they are helping. President Thomas Jefferson, son of a land surveyor, has sent out the Corps of Discovery to claim western North America for the United States. The fact that

MAPPING OFF PAPER

The peoples of Africa, Australia, the far north, and the Americas did not produce paper charts, for a simple reason: such maps weren't useful to them.

The Ammassalik people of Greenland had to find their way in a land that is dark in winter months, where they couldn't walk in a straight line from A to B if the ice in between was treacherous or the way blocked by huge ridges of snow. For them, paper maps of fixed positions would have been useless. So they developed the right kind of map for their landscape and their way of life. They carved the outlines of their land, its cliffs and bays and hills, onto pieces of wood. These relief maps could be read by feel, in the winter darkness or in a blinding snowstorm.

Many of the Native peoples encountered by European explorers in North America were nomadic hunters. It would make no sense for them to draw the outlines of their territories, because the outlines were always shifting as they moved through the land following animals for food. It made more sense to use "mental maps" – songs and stories – to tell about routes and the locations of dangers, good hunting grounds, and sacred places. Then they could tell these stories to guide their families on their way.

Nomadic peoples could produce cartographic maps if they wanted to. The great French explorer of North America Samuel de Champlain reported in 1611 that the Native people along the St. Lawrence River "told me many things, both of the rivers, falls, lakes and lands, and of the tribes living there . . . showing me by drawings all the places that they had visited."

people such as the Mandans have lived there for thousands of years doesn't matter, since they have no officially recognized maps or surveys giving them legal claim. Lewis and Clark have come to survey the land for settlement by white people.

On November 11, 1804, Clark writes in his journal about the arrival in Mandan lands of a fur-trader from Montreal, named Charbonneau, and his teenage wife. This girl, a Shoshone, was kidnapped when she was about eleven by the Hidatsa people, who sold her to the fur-trader. Now she is pregnant. Her name is Sacagawea.

Lewis and Clark size up Charbonneau, and decide he is shifty and bad-tempered. But they figure that his wife might be useful as an interpreter when their expedition gets to Shoshone country. They offer to hire Charbonneau for the journey west – if he brings along Sacagawea.

The Mandan were not suspicious of the white mapmakers because they didn't even think of the land, or use it, in the same terms as Europeans. For Native peoples, land was to be hunted in, traveled over, and praised. "What is this thing you call property?" Massasoit, a chief of the Wampanoag country, had asked colonists in the place the newcomers called New England. "It cannot be the Earth, for the land is our mother. The woods, the streams, everything on it belongs to everybody. How can one man say it belongs only to him?"

For Europeans, land was something to be controlled, divided up, sold, taxed, and developed. Land hunger was one big reason why the United States was born. In 1763, when King George III of England ordered colonists to stop settling west of the Appalachian Mountains, the colonists rebelled. After the Americans gained independence, they realized that if they didn't plant their flag in the west, the British would. The British had been sniffing around ever since James Cook and George Vancouver hoisted the British Union Jack along the Pacific Coast in the 18th century.

THE MAPMAKERS' SENSE OF THE LAND

Today's map of Lewis and Clark's North America.

There were British explorers moving in by land, too – such as Alexander Mackenzie, a Scots-Canadian mapmaker and fur-trader. Guided by Nuxalk Natives, he traveled down the Bella Coola River to the Pacific at the end of the 18th century. To impress other Europeans that he was the first European to cross the continent, he fixed his position by latitude and longitude and, on a rock overlooking the Pacific, used vermilion and grease to paint this sign: *Alexander Mackenzie from Canada, by land, the 22nd of July 1793.* On his return to England, Mackenzie wrote a book about his achievement. American President Thomas Jefferson read it with great interest, aware that other Canadian fur-traders were planning on following Mackenzie. In 1801, David Thompson, who knew Mackenzie, had already tried to find a way through the Rocky Mountains near present-day Banff, Alberta. So it was with a sense of urgency that Jefferson ordered Lewis, Clark, and their team of forty men to set sail from St. Louis, Missouri, in May 1804.

The group included Clark's slave — a man named York — and several Métis woodsmen — part French-Canadian, part Aboriginal. The group's mission was to explore the west, to find an overland route to the Pacific, and to note which lands would be good for settlement. They brought along rough maps of the regions into which they were heading, which showed one ridge of mountains and about 3,000 kilometers (2,000 miles) of unmapped land between themselves and the Pacific. They figured the trip would take about a year.

As they sailed up the river, the Corps of Discovery would stop at Native villages and call a council. To impress everyone, the Americans showed off their magnets, spyglasses, and guns. Then they would smoke pipes, and trade needles and buttons in exchange for food and information. York was part of the show too — he had to stand around and let Native people who had never seen a black man before run their curious hands over his kinky hair and dark skin.

Sometimes the expedition passed deserted villages. Already, contact with European fur-traders had brought smallpox to the west, and thousands of Native people had died. Still, the people along the Missouri could see that Lewis and Clark, with their questions and peace pipes and trading goods, weren't on a war mission. Besides, Clark used his skills in Western medicine to cure the sick.

In February 1804, in the middle of their long winter with the Mandan, Clark used those skills to help Sacagawea give birth to a little

As seen on this one-dollar American coin, Sacagawea was a young mother. There are more statues of Sacagawea in the U.S. than of any other woman. She is usually shown pointing west.

boy named Jean-Baptiste. Before the baby was two months old, spring came and lifted the ice from the Missouri River. The Mandan village began to stir with rumors that British fur-traders were riling up Native people against the Americans. They heard news that the Spanish of New Mexico, fearing that the Americans would take over Spanish territory, and had sent a raiding party of fierce Comanches to stop them. It was time to get moving.

Sacagawea strapped the baby onto a cradleboard, hoisted him on her back, and followed the expedition up the river into what is now Montana. They sailed past huge herds of bison and astonishing rock formations. Wherever they landed, the new mother helped out by finding prairie roots and berries to add to the expedition dinners.

On May 14, a sudden squall tipped the boat, and dumped the expedition's equipment, medicines, journals, and trading goods into the river. Charbonneau panicked, and another Métis threatened to shoot him if he didn't calm down. Meanwhile Sacagawea quietly collected the floating equipment and laid it on the bank to dry. Lewis wrote, "The Indian woman, to whom I ascribe equal fortitude and resolution with any person . . . caught and preserved most of the articles." A few weeks later, Sacagawea fell ill. Clark nursed her with a rich soup made of bison meat.

The explorers were starting to realize that the west was far more vast than their rough maps had indicated. They charted as they went, making notes about the landscape's beauty ("The hills we passed today exhibit a most romantic appearance"), but they realized with sinking hearts that there was no chance of reaching the Pacific and returning home again within a year.

By midsummer they came to the Missouri headwaters — the rivers beyond flowed westward to the Pacific. On July 22, Sacagawea cheered up everyone by announcing that she recognized Shoshone country. Lewis (who was a terrible speller) wrote in his journal, "She is our only dependence for a friendly negociation with the Snake [Shoshone] Indians on whom we depend for horses to assist us in our portage from the Missouri to the Columbia river."

A week later they met their first Shoshone, a warrior on horseback who invited them to his village. Sacagawea, normally reserved and calm, began "to show every mark of the most extravagant joy." As the travelers seated themselves in the tent of Chief Cameahwait, Sacagawea prepared to translate. Suddenly she jumped up, hugged Cameahwait, and burst into tears. He was her brother. She had not seen him since she was kidnapped as a girl.

Chief Cameahwait gave the expedition horses and guides, and the Corps of Discovery bade the Shoshone farewell. Again, Sacagawea picked up young Jean-Baptiste and followed. As sister of the chief, she could have stayed among her people. But perhaps she figured that her baby would have a better chance with Clark as doctor and protector. Maybe the Americans

DAVID THOMPSON

Canada's greatest mapmaker was fourteen when he kissed his mother goodbye and sailed from London to Canada to work for the Hudson's Bay Company. David Thompson never saw his mother again.

The boy spent his first winters in the 1780s in a fort on the desolate Churchill River, reading poetry and learning to speak Native languages. The Hudson's Bay Company trained him to survey and measure longitude and latitude by sighting heavenly bodies, so his Native friends called him Koo-Koo-sint, or "the man who looks at stars." In 1793 Thompson mapped the lands west of Hudson's Bay and, in 1798, the Mandan lands of the Dakotas.

The next year, he took a half-Cree teenager, Charlotte Small, as his wife. White men often abandoned their Native wives and families when they returned to Europe, but Thompson was different. Charlotte and their children even accompanied him on some of his explorations of the Rockies.

In 1811, he found a route through the mountains to the Columbia River, which he charted as it tumbled to the sea. But when Thompson emerged out of the forest, he saw the Stars and Stripes flying over Fort Astoria at the river's mouth. Thompson was too late to claim the land for England, but his accomplishments are remarkable. In his twenty-seven years in the fur trade, he made beautiful, accurate maps of North America's northwest, covering some 80,000 km^2 (50,000 square miles). His journals are fascinating accounts of living among the Native peoples. As for his own family, when he retired from the fur trade in 1812, he took them all back east, and married Charlotte for a second time.

begged her to come along. Probably she was curious to see the world.

But the going was rough. Each time the Corps of Discovery climbed to the top of a mountain ridge, they expected to see the sea in the distance. Each time, they saw more white-capped mountains along the horizon. In September, it began to snow. Food grew scarce and they had to kill some of the horses to eat.

Coming down from the heights, the expedition entered the semi-desert lands of the Nez Perce people. On white elkskin, the Nez Perce drew maps of the rivers that lay ahead: the Clearwater, which flows into the Snake, which flows into the Columbia, which flows to the Pacific. As they journeyed, Sacagawea was their goodwill ambassador, wrote Clark: "The sight of this woman assured people of our friendly intentions."

By November 1805, the weather got damper and the forests thick and dark. The group knew they must be nearing the sea. Lewis and Clark asked the other members of the expedition to vote on where they should spend the winter. York the slave voted — six decades before black people got the vote in the United States. Sacagawea voted too — more than one hundred years before most North American women could legally vote.

The group voted to stay in a grove of pines near the site of present-day Astoria, Oregon, and built a wooden fort, which they named Fort Clatsop. At Christmas, a delighted Clark wrote that Sacagawea gave him "two dozens white weazils tails" (there is no mention of her giving anything to Lewis). For Christmas dinner they all dined on rotten elk meat.

Early in 1806, some Native people visiting the fort mentioned that a huge whale lay dead on a beach not far away. As the men prepared to go and see, Sacagawea made the only complaint she voiced for the entire expedition. She had come a very long way, she said, hoping to see the great waters of the ocean. "And now that monstrous fish was also to be seen, she thought it very hard she could not be permitted to see either." Clark agreed to bring his curious comrade along.

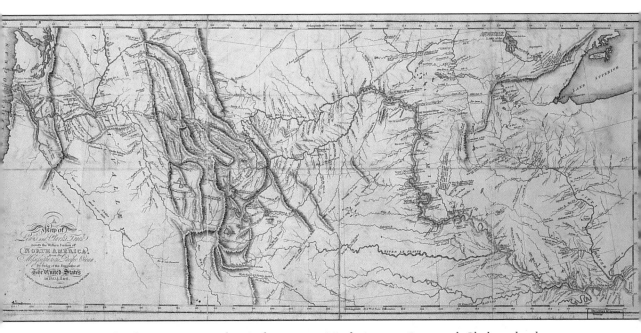

On their return from the expedition across North America, Lewis and Clark produced a map. It revealed the major difficulty of their journey. Not one range of mountains lay between the Missouri River and the sea, but three: the Rockies, the Cascades, and the Coastals.

Through the winter days, Lewis and Clark worked on their journals and on transferring compass readings and latitude and longitude measurements to larger maps.

In the spring of 1806, the Corps of Discovery left Fort Clatsop and headed back east. Sacagawea picked up her boy, Jean-Baptiste, now a heavy toddler, and followed once more. This time the group found easier routes. Clark wrote, "The Indian woman, who has been of great service to me as a pilot through this country, recommends a gap in the mountains more south, which I shall cross."

By August they were back among the Mandans, where Charbonneau and his wife left the expedition. Lewis and Clark paid Charbonneau $500 in wages. Although they had found that his wife was "particularly useful," they did not pay Sacagawea. However, Clark later adopted Jean-Baptiste. When Sacagawea's son grew up, he went to Europe and worked for a

German prince. Most accounts say Sacagawea died of a fever around 1812.

Back in the east, Lewis and Clark were greeted with honor and fame. Clark married, named his eldest son after Meriwether Lewis, and lived to a ripe old age. But after Clark's wedding, Lewis fell into a depression. He missed the glory days, and his friend. He was unable to finish his journals. In 1809, he died of shotgun wounds — probably suicide.

The maps these men made profoundly changed traditional Native life. North American land would never again belong to everybody. Captured by lines of latitude and longitude, western North America was jerked from Aboriginal to white hands. After the explorers, a new kind of mapmaker followed — surveyors carrying measuring chains and posts, which they drove into the earth to mark the boundaries of new townships, so the land could be sold to white settlers.

So the maps of North America kept changing. No longer did people sketch wild rivers into the ashes of campfires, or draw on elkskins to show great hunting grounds. And they didn't transfer exploration notes onto maps of a vast wilderness. Instead, people made real estate charts showing property lines, town lots, and ranches. Then came roadmaps showing highways connecting sprawling new cities. The charts of Thompson and Lewis and Clark — maps scribbled by the light of campfires somewhere in a vast wilderness — were put in archives and museums to sit alongside the maps of the Native peoples.

But the story of North American mapmaking is not over. The latest chapter is like the story of a ghost who comes to life again.

In 1987, two British Columbia Aboriginal nations, the Gitksan — led by Ken Muldoe, or Delgamuukw — and the Wet'suwet'en, took the British Columbian and Canadian governments to court to claim their ancestral lands. They asked the Lower Court to consider the traditional Aboriginal stories as "oral maps" that would establish their claim on the land. The Lower Court decided that such song-and-story maps were vague, and were concerned that the territories they described often over-lapped. The Court ruled against the Native nations.

But Delgamuukw and his fellow claimants appealed to the Supreme Court of Canada. In 1996, in a landmark case now known as the Delgamuukw Decision, the Canadian Supreme Court agreed that oral traditional maps had to be considered along with European-style maps. Since the Delgamuukw precedent was set, other nations have been able to use their oral maps to win back land. For example, the Nisga'a have regained control of 120,000 km² (46,000 square miles) of the Lower Nass River Valley in British Columbia.

So those Aboriginal maps aren't dead after all. They have just been sleeping — and some are starting to awake.

THE UNDERSEA MAPMAKERS

Mapping the Ocean Depths

IT IS A brilliant day off the Azores Islands, and the H.M.S. Challenger, a British Royal Navy ship, is taking up her first station, or fixed position. From here, her crew will measure the speed of the ocean's current and the water's temperature, and will take samples of the sea bottom. As gentle trade winds try to blow the Challenger eastward, she uses her engines to hold steady, to allow the scientists to take their first readings. According to what the ship's chemist, John Buchanan, will later write, the science of oceanography does not exist until this point: "It may be taken that the science of Oceanography was born at Sea, at Latitude 25 degrees 45 minutes North, Longitude 20 degrees, 14 minutes west on 15th February 1873 . . . . "

It takes hours for the Challenger's lines to spool out. The winch makes an annoying grinding noise (over the next three years the crew will grow to hate it). It takes another four hours to haul up the dredge from the ocean floor 5 kilometers (3.5 miles) below. In late afternoon, John Murray, a curly-haired Canadian medical student from Cobourg, Ontario, joins everyone else on deck to see the dredge open its mechanical jaws and drop out 45 kilograms (100 pounds) of reddish, lifeless clay.

What a disappointment, Murray must have said to himself. *Is the bottom of the sea really so dull?*

Humans have sailed across the seas for thousands of years, but for most of that time knew little of what was below. The average depth of the shallowest ocean, the Indian, is almost 4,000 meters (13,000 feet). It's dark down there, and the pressure of all the water would crush a mapmaker and his instruments.

Only in the late 19th century did we start to chart the oceans. As nations began laying underwater telegraph cables, the need for accurate maps of the ocean floor began to grow. American, British, French, German, and Scandinavian expeditions set out to do the job.

In 1752, a French mapmaker, Philippe Buache, made a chart showing the contour lines of the floor of the English Channel. In 1855, Matthew Maury, director of the U.S. Navy's Depot of Charts, used soundings, or depth measurements, given to him by whaling ships and his own naval vessels to produce the first contour map of the Atlantic sea floor. Maury detected an undersea ridge in the mid-Atlantic, which he named Middle Ground or Dolphin Rise. But Maury's information was limited. To make his bathymetrical map of the Atlantic, he had used only 200 soundings of regions that were deeper than 1000 fathoms (1.8 km/1 mile), and his chart was dotted with question marks.

In fact, scientists had many questions about what lived in the deepest seas. A respected English naturalist, Edward Forbes, declared that the depths were frigid, dark, and empty — "zero of life." But Charles Darwin, the father of evolutionary science, insisted that the sea held the secrets of life's origins.

In 1871, the U.S. sent out a deep-sea expedition — it wasn't a success, but that's another story. English national pride bristled. A professor at the University of Edinburgh, Wyville Thomson, scolded the British

THE PRINCE AND THE SEA

Prince Albert, heir to the throne of Monaco, was disappointed that France was not leading the way in sea exploration. Although he lacked the resources of the U.S. Navy or the Challenger expedition, he joined the race to chart the ocean depths. In September 1873, Prince Albert set out in his schooner Hirondelle (Swallow), to show what one imaginative individual could do. Off the Azores, he threw overboard glass bottles and beer barrels containing messages asking anyone who found one to return it with news about where the sea currents had carried it. Over the next few years the Prince released more bottles off England and Newfoundland – a total of almost 1,700 bottles. Only 227 were ever returned. But they showed that the North Atlantic current flows clockwise, from the Gulf of Mexico northwards, then across the Atlantic to the British Isles, where one stream peels away to the north while the other turns south and crosses the Atlantic again. During World War I, Prince Albert predicted that German mines that broke loose along the European coast would be carried westward across the Atlantic and then back to Europe. Sure enough, more than sixty mines that had followed that route were recovered.

Another of Prince Albert's low-tech strategies for ocean study occurred to him one day off Africa when he harpooned a whale. The wounded beast charged the Hirondelle, but died just before smashing into it. Then its great mouth opened and out floated the remains of its last meal, eaten in the deep. Prince Albert stared in fascination. "What precious regurgitations!" he shouted. He ordered lifeboats over the side to scoop up all the whale vomit they could. In the mess, he discovered five new species of squid. By checking out the vomit of dead whales, the prince had a low-cost, organic dredge.

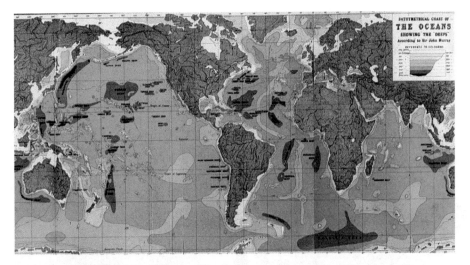

The "Bathymetrical Chart of the World's Oceans, according to Sir John Murray" was produced two decades after the Challenger's historic voyage. The Challenger made 364 stops to gather sea-bottom samples and take depth soundings, but Sir John also used additional information from other ocean-going ships to make this map.

government for "leaving everything to our rivals to gather up. Is this creditable to the Power which claims to be Mistress of the Seas?"

Alarmed, the British government agreed to equip a navy corvette, the H.M.S. Challenger, with state-of-the-art laboratories and a steam-driven winch to pull up a deep-sea dredge. The crew included Wyville Thomson and his young Canadian student John Murray, who joined the expedition at the last minute. Their mission: to find out all they could about the currents and geography of the sea; to study marine life forms; and to find out if the deepest parts of the sea really were "zero of life."

On December 21, 1872, the Challenger sailed from England for the Azores, performed her first, disappointing dredging, and then headed across the Atlantic. In March, off the West Indies, she did her second deep-sea dredge — another day of listening to the winch grinding down, down, down, and then up, up, up with another enormous mouthful of muck.

This time, as the sailors washed masses of sea-bottom mud through

This woodcut from the fifty-volume Challenger Report shows the H.M.S. Challenger preparing to take a depth measurement. Challenger carried 230 kilometers (144 miles) of hemp rope and 20 kilometers (12 miles) of piano wire to make depth soundings.

sieves, something lumpy refused to pass through. A shout went up. Everyone gathered round. Had humans ever before been so happy, so thrilled, to see . . . worms? There they were, from the greatest depth of the ocean yet dredged, creatures that lived inside tubes of mucus-hardened sand. Floppy, glistening, repulsive – but unmistakably alive.

Now that they had put to rest the idea that the ocean depths were "zero of life," the Challenger crew continued to measure water temperatures and speed of the ocean currents. On land, water tends to flow across a surface. In the sea, a current flows up and down more freely. The scientists onboard noticed that in the eastern North Atlantic, the deep-sea temperatures were warmer by several degrees than water at the same depth in the same latitude in the Atlantic off North America. Was there some sort of wall dividing the sea down where Maury had marked Dolphin Rise? The Challenger scientists had no idea how big this wall would prove to be.

By early 1874, when the Challenger turned into the Pacific, John Murray was the ship's expert in sea bottoms. When the dredge coughed up new muck from the ocean floor he would rub it to see if it was gritty or greasy. He would sniff it and even taste it. Like a wine snob, he could tell you almost exactly where a sample was from. Tomato-red clay was

These marine worms from the sea bottom are depicted in a 19th-century German book on oceanography, Das Meer.

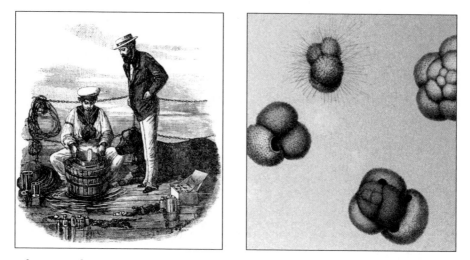

The crew and scientists aboard the H.M.S. Challenger sifted deposits from the depths of both the Atlantic and Pacific oceans. They found specimens of many forms of life (like those illustrated above right) that were completely unknown until then.

found deep in the south Atlantic, while from off Australia came liquorice-black lumps – bits of coral coated with a veneer of manganese.

But even Murray was unprepared for the deep-sea sounding one day off Guam in the Pacific. For several days the Challenger had been sailing above 2,300 fathoms. On this day, when the scientists lowered the line, it kept spooling. It unwound past the 4,000-fathom (7-km/4.5-mile) mark, then 4,500 fathoms (8 km/5 miles). Had the lengthening line somehow been swept sideways by a strong current? Finally it stopped – at 4,575 fathoms or 8.5 kilometers (5.3 miles). The Challenger was above one of the deepest places on Earth, what's now known as the Challenger Deep, at one end of the great Marianas Trench. Parts of the Trench are 6,000 fathoms, or 11 kilometers (7 miles) down.

When the line was finally pulled up and its deposits examined under Challenger's microscopes, the scientists found tiny shells in the red clay. They were learning that the ocean supports life at all levels.

In 1876, the Challenger returned to England. She had sailed 111,000

THE UNDERSEA MAPMAKERS

kilometers (68,930 miles), returning with 1,441 water samples and 13,000 new sea-plants and sea-animals.

Young John Murray took over the job of writing up the fifty-volume Challenger *Report* (the full title was *Report on the scientific results of the voyage of H.M.S. Challenger during the years 1873-76 under the command of Captain George S. Nares, R.N., F.R.S. and the late Captain Frank Tourle Thomson, R.N*). Murray made a lot of money turning phosphates from Pacific islands into fertilizers, and he used his fortune to support more undersea expeditions. He continued to collect samples of sea-bottom muck from everyone else who went dredging, including telegraph companies laying submarine cables. In 1886 he published the first topographical maps of the Atlantic, Pacific, and Indian Oceans. His most comprehensive map of the sea bottoms came out in 1895, in the final (50th) volume of the Challenger *Report*. By the time Sir John published his book *The Depths of the Oceans* in 1912, he had studied more than 11,000 samples of sea sediment.

John Murray was knighted for his contributions to oceanography and our knowledge of the nature of the ocean floor.

"SOUNDING" THE DEEPS

For as long as sailors have run their ships aground, people have understood the importance of measuring and charting the water's depths. For thousands of years, this was done using a lead-line – a rope with a lead weight at the end – that was lowered over the side of the boat while sailors watched how far it spooled down. As recently as the 19th century, surveys of the ocean floor were being done by dropping lines over a boat's side and taking depth soundings.

In 1912, the Titanic hit an iceberg and went down off eastern Canada. To help sea captains detect icebergs, a Canadian inventor named Reginald Fessenden, one of the pioneers of radio, came up with an oscillator that could produce an underwater sound wave. Just as echolocation helps bats and dolphins find their way, Fessenden's sound waves could detect big underwater shapes, such as mountain ranges, in the darkest reaches of the sea. Sonar revolutionized underwater mapping.

In 1899, Murray joined Prince Albert of Monaco and scientists from more than a dozen countries for an International Geographical Congress, called to come up with a standard map of the oceans. Prince Albert took on the work – and the cost – of compiling all the latest charts, including Sir John's topographical maps of the oceans. The Prince also founded the International Hydrographic Bureau, headquartered in Monaco, to keep the charts updated. It's still there, hard at work.

With the development of sonar in the early 20th century, oceanographers had a new tool with which to map the depths. Prince Albert was a pioneer of sonic mapping before his death in 1922. In the 1930s, a British

expedition named after John Murray charted the Arabian Sea with sonar, and detected a long undersea mountain range that seemed divided, or cleft.

World War II halted exploration again. Then, in the late 1940s, Maurice Ewing of Columbia University and his assistant Bruce Hezeen took sonar readings of the mid-Atlantic, the area once called Dolphin Rise. Ewing and Hezeen took their data to their colleague Marie Tharp, who in 1953 began plotting the data on charts.

Soon Tharp was puzzling over the same kind of strange mountain ranges – cleft in the middle – that the British scientists on the John Murray Expedition had noticed. In places this cleft was as deep as the Grand Canyon. For months, Tharp couldn't convince Ewing and Hezeen to take a closer look. When they finally did, they realized they were looking at something really big: in fact, the sea bottom revealed how the

Shown at the far left, Prince Albert holds a shark when the day's catch of specimens is displayed.

planet was formed. The clefts showed where huge plates had collided, pushing up into double mountain ranges.

The map Tharp and Hezeen brought out in 1957, a portrait of how the sea bottom would look like if drained of water, revolutionized geography. For the first time, humans could see the huge, M-shaped mountain range running down the middle of the Atlantic Ocean — and the Arctic, Antarctic, Indian, and Pacific Oceans, too. This mountain range is 65,000 kilometers (40,000 miles) long. It encircles the whole Earth. It has been pushed up, and pulled apart, along the edges of the plates of the surface of the Earth. As the plates shift, earthquakes occur, and trenches like the Marianas Trench are formed. Where the edges stretch apart, volcanoes burst through — sometimes forming islands. The Mid-Oceanic Range, as it's now known, is one world-circling belt of rubbing, grinding tensions that shapes the planet on which we live.

The seas cover three-quarters of the Earth's surface. We lived in the dark about the secrets of the deep — and the mysteries of how the Earth was formed — until people such as Prince Albert and Sir John Murray mapped the part of the world that lay hidden under the waves.

THE MAPMAKER'S DISGUISE

Secret Maps

IT IS EARLY in 1865, and a caravan plods through the cold, rocky passes of southern Tibet. It is heading for the capital, Lhasa, one of the highest and most remote cities in the world. Most people in the caravan are merchants, carrying cotton and tobacco to barter for Tibetan wool, borax, and goats. But one man is dressed as a Buddhist pilgrim. The other travelers think he must be very pious, for he walks thoughtfully, always handling his rosary beads and murmuring the Buddhist prayer "Om Mani Padme Hum" ("Hail, Jewel of the Lotus!")

If the merchants were to look more closely, they might notice something odd. Instead of the usual 108 beads, this pilgrim's rosary has an even hundred, and every tenth bead is slightly larger than the rest. They might see him slip tiny pieces of paper into the cracks in his prayer wheel. If they examined his prayer wheel, they might find that it unscrews to reveal a compass. His pilgrim's staff conceals a miniature thermometer. Fortunately for Pundit Nain Singh, no one ever checks.

Singh is no holy man. His British spymasters call him Number 1 and, like the fictional 007, he is equipped with top-secret equipment, charm, and the guts to defy death.

QUILT MAPS

You are a slave in the 1800s, and you are running for your life through a forest somewhere in the southern United States. The yelps of the tracking dogs and the sound of the slave catchers crashing through the undergrowth are getting closer. Up ahead, outside a cabin, hangs a quilt. You can just make out its pattern – a sailboat. It's a sign, and you can read it. It says you must cross a body of water. Sure enough, there's a river up ahead, and a small raft waiting. You take the raft to the far shore, and off you run again. The yelping dies away. As night falls, you scan the sky and find the Big Dipper. Also called the Drinking Gourd, the constellation points you to the North Star. You hum the song "Follow the Drinking Gourd" as you head north towards freedom.

Before the end of slavery in the United States, about 60,000 black people escaped from southern slave states to free states and to Canada. Runaways could not carry maps, which might give them away, and they were forbidden to learn how to read anyway. So their maps to freedom were "mental maps" coded in the words of songs and in patterns on quilts. What kind of directions could a quilt map give? A zigzag pattern known as the Drunkard's Path was a sign that you should move the way a drunk person moves, back and forth instead of in a straight line. The Crossroads pattern was a symbol for the city of Cleveland, Ohio. And if you saw a quilt with a log cabin on it and a black center, you could be pretty sure that here was a safe place to rest.

This map of the Vale of Kashmir was made around 1836 by Abdur Rahim (who was from modern-day Uzbekistan). It was purchased by a British army captain, whose bosses were thrilled to have a map of a region "beyond our frontiers."

By the last half of the 19th century the British, who controlled India, had also mapped most of it — except for the far north, where the world's tallest mountains, the Himalayas, blocked the way. The way was also blocked by the Russians, who were keenly interested in central Asia. The Chinese knew that if the Russians or British got maps of the region, it would give them a way to extend their influence there. So the Emperor of China decreed that no foreigner, especially a European, should enter Tibet unauthorized — on pain of death.

The British leaders of the Great Indian Survey, perhaps the most ambitious mapping project undertaken to that time, weren't going to leave the top of their map blank. They had purchased whatever maps they could from local people, but they wanted more accurate data. If English survey-ors could not enter Tibet, then English-trained surveyors must do the job.

The man they needed taught school in the Johar Valley near India's border with present-day Nepal. A slim thirty-year-old, Pandit Nain Singh (*pandit* or *pundit* means "learned man") was the son of a trader who had taught him some of the Tibetan language. In 1863 Singh agreed to accept the most dangerous job in the Great Indian Survey, and went to its northern headquarters at Dehra Dun to train.

For two years he studied the use of surveying tools: theodolite, sextant, compass, and thermometer (to calculate altitude). But Singh's basic tools were his feet. For two years he practiced pacing so that he could walk a mile in precisely 2,000 steps, each step around 79 centimeters (31 inches).

Singh set off in January 1865, eventually joining a caravan traveling across the cold, stony plateau towards Lhasa. By October the caravan reached Shigatse. There Singh learned, to his alarm, that they would be presented to the Panchan Lama, a religious leader said to have the power to see deep into men's hearts. The spy was taken to the lama. But if the gorgeously robed boy on the Panchan throne saw through Singh's disguise, he didn't show it. His Holiness merely blessed Singh and offered him tea.

On the caravan went towards Lhasa. As Number 1 paced 2,000 steps to the mile, he fingered his special rosary beads, marking every thousand paces. In secret, he wrote down the distance he had traveled and the coor-dinates of his present location, slipping his notes into his prayer wheel. Using his secret thermometer to take the temperature of water he boiled for tea, he was able to calculate altitude at more than thirty sites.

In January 1866, the mapmaker walked into the walled city of Lhasa. His calculations put it at an altitude of 3,475 meters (11,400 feet) — pretty close to its correct height of 3,600 meters (11,800 feet). Here he survived for three months like a typical pilgrim, holding out his begging bowl for strangers to fill with food.

THE MAPMAKER'S DISGUISE

Map Showing the
Route Survey from
NEPAL TO LHASA
and thence through the
UPPER VALLEY OF THE BRAHMAPUTRA
Made by: Pundit
from the Map compiled by Capt. T.G. Montgomerie R.E.

The survey notes of the brave and clever Pundit Nain Singh enabled a member of the Great Indian Survey, Captain T.G. Montgomerie, to compile this map of Nepal (left) and Tibet (upper right) in 1868.

While Number 1 stayed in Lhasa, he was always in danger. He saw the Chinese publicly beheading people not authorized to be in the forbidden city. By April, the mapmaker decided it was time to escape. He joined a westward-bound caravan. As they traveled out of Tibet, he charted their 800-kilometer (500-mile) route along the Tsangpo River. One night, he slipped away into the dark and headed back to Dehra Dun.

The British spymasters were delighted with Singh's reports of his 1,900-kilometer (1,200-mile) journey, and with his measurements of altitude and latitude. They declared that he had "added a greater amount of positive knowledge to the map of Asia than any individual of our time." Number 1 was made a Companion of the Indian Empire, and given medals and a pension for life.

But there was this problem: Singh had brought back not only answers to questions on the map, but a new question as well. Did the Tsangpo River flow through the mountains to become the mighty Brahmaputra River? To solve the mystery, the spymasters came up with an ingenious

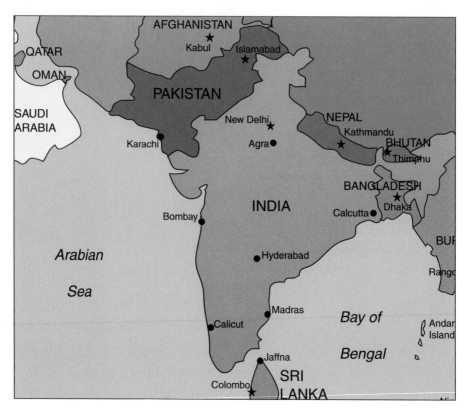

Today's map of Singh's and Kinthup's India.

plan. They would send another Indian team into the Himalayas to float fifty logs a day for ten days down the Tsangpo. If fifty logs a day turned up on the Brahmaputra, the two rivers must be one.

This time they recruited a real holy man, or lama, for the journey, and gave him a servant named Kinthup to help with the secret mapmaking. In 1880, the two headed into the mountains. Unfortunately, the lama turned out to be a scoundrel. He used his pay to get drunk, and sometimes beat his servant Kinthup. The last straw came when he sold Kinthup into slavery in a Tibetan village, and vanished.

The long-suffering Kinthup worked for the village boss for two years. Finally he escaped and headed up the Tsangpo River, determined

THE MAPMAKER'S DISGUISE

to finish the job his boss had abandoned. With slave-catchers out looking for him, Kinthup hid in a monastery for four months. Then he slipped away into the forest and cut down trees until he had 500 logs. He

SECRET MAPS

Maps offer information, and information is power. So maps have a long history of spies, lies, and disguise. In the days of Henry the Navigator, the Portuguese tried to keep their knowledge of Africa to themselves. But Dutch and Italian agents managed to steal copies. So did the English pirate Sir Walter Raleigh – and possibly Christopher Columbus, whose brother worked in the Portuguese map library.

In the 16th century, the Russians executed anyone convicted of selling maps of Siberia, the remotest regions of Russia. The Hudson's Bay Company kept its archives of Canadian charts closed to the public until the late 18th century.

In the 20th century, when the Soviet Union feared that the West might try to invade and topple its Communist government, it produced maps that showed strategic cities hundreds of miles away from their true location. During World War II, the British government doctored aerial photo maps by hand-painting fields over airports and factories. Sometimes the British map-disguisers put cotton balls on top of photos of secret sites, and then photographed the photographs, so that the cotton balls looked like clouds covering part of the landscape.

Today, the U.S. government tries to limit the publication of sensitive satellite images. And just try getting your hands on a hiker's-scale map of China's hotly disputed Tibet border!

dragged them to the river and, every day for ten days, tossed in fifty logs so the British watching downstream would see them.

But two long years had passed, and the British back in India had given up watching. Had they stayed at their posts they would have seen the logs, for the Tsangpo does indeed become the Brahmaputra. But there was nobody there to see.

When Kinthup finally turned up in India after a four-year absence, his spymasters were shamed by his dedication to a job they had abandoned. He was honored and his name is still a symbol of devotion to duty among Indian mapmakers.

It is a testament to our continuing faith in the power of maps that some people try so hard to keep their contents secret — and others risk their lives to fill in their blank spaces.

THE MAPMAKER AND HER BUSINESS

Phyllis Pearsall

IT IS A RAINY night in London, England, in 1935. Phyllis Pearsall, a portrait painter, has taken the wrong bus. She is lost. She was on her way to the house of her old school friend, Lady Veronica Knott, but London's streets are confusing, and no one Phyllis asks knows the right way. When she finally arrives at Lady Veronica's door, Phyllis is very wet and very late.

"Of course it is impossible to find your way in London without a taxi," says Lady Veronica, pampering the dripping Phyllis with a glass of wine and a dinner of roast duck. Phyllis promises herself that the very next day she will get herself a good, up-to-date street map of London. The next day, she discovers that there isn't one. And so Phyllis, a divorced woman with very little money, decides to make one. It is the start of her fortune.

Phyllis Isobelle Gross was born in Dulwich, London, in 1906, to a rich, unhappy family. Her charming, difficult father, Alexander "Sandor" Gross, was a Jew who had left small-town Hungary to make his fortune in England. He and his wife, Bella, started a business publishing maps and worked like demons to make it succeed. Their

CONSUMER MAPS

Different people need different maps. Consumer maps, like the ones sold by Geographia, are for ordinary people with no special training in mathematics or geography. Often they are cartograms, or simplified diagrams. One classic cartogram is the map of the London subway, drawn in 1933 by Harry Beck. Beck realized that an accurate map of London's complicated Underground would be a big tangle of crisscrossing tracks. His simplified map is all straight lines and 45-degree angles, and each subway line has a different color code. Beck spaced the stations not where they actually were, but where the lettering of their names could be read most clearly. His subway map has been imitated by subway systems all over the world, including New York, Washington, and Toronto. It also had a nice side effect: it boosted subway passenger traffic enormously, as people felt more confident about finding their way.

Geographia company published roadmaps for drivers of the newly invented motorcars. It was the first company in England to make aerial maps for those who traveled by an even newer invention, the airplane. Geographia also made maps to be published in newspapers, showing everything from the routes of royal funerals to where battles were taking place in World War I.

Sandor and Bella made a lot of money and sent their children, Phyllis and Tony, to expensive schools. But, at first, Phyllis found it hard to win friends at her school, Roedean. The meanest girls called Phyllis "Pig" (for her initials, **Phyllis Isobelle Gross**). But she was good at art and won the school geography prize. Then one day, when Phyllis was thirteen, she was hauled out of class, to be told that she would have to leave the school because her parents' company had gone broke.

Phyllis was sent back to London, where she learned that Sandor and Bella had been spending more than they earned. The war was changing the boundaries of Europe so fast, Geographia's maps were out-of-date and the company had started to lose money. Sandor blamed everyone but himself. He fired his wife, who ran off with an alcoholic painter. Then Sandor left London too, to start a new mapmaking business in America.

At first Phyllis lived with her grandparents and supported herself by working as a tutor. Her brother Tony became an artist and moved to Paris. Phyllis followed him, but was too proud to ask Tony if she could sleep on his floor. She slept under bridges, wrapping herself in newspapers for warmth.

Luckily Phyllis was clever and talented, and soon found she could make money by writing newspaper articles and selling paintings. In 1929, she married an artist friend of Tony's named Dick Pearsall. Unfortunately Dick got jealous when Phyllis's paintings sold better than his did. After six years, Phyllis left him. But she kept his name; as Phyllis Pearsall, she would no longer be "Pig."

Sandor Gross wanted everyone to see how far he had come fron the Hungarian village of Csurog. He even bought a pet elephant for his children, shown here with Phyllis as a child.

Back again in London, she had to earn a living. Her father had become rich publishing maps of New York, but Phyllis had no intention of working for Sandor — she didn't want to risk being pushed aside as her mother had been. Phyllis decided on a different career — painting portraits of her old school chums. With her vibrant sense of color and line, and her stories about life in romantic Paris, Phyllis did well. Her friends happily paid her to paint them and often invited her for dinner as well. Which is what Lady Veronica Knott did that night in 1935.

It was odd that Phyllis was unable to find a good London map. People had mapped London for more than 2,000 years, since Roman times. A map from the year 1217 by the English monk Matthew Paris shows the city in such detail, you can see the Tower of London. In 1627, John Speed published a pocket-sized map of London that was a bestseller.

But London had kept growing and changing. So in 1935, what Phyllis Pearsall wanted was not available. There was no map that showed the complicated city of seven million people, with subways and new developments, where some streets had no numbers and others shared identical names. The most complete map of London, Phyllis discovered, was the army's Ordnance Survey map (showing military locations), published in 1919.

Phyllis phoned her father in New York and said she wanted to publish a new guide to London. Sandor Gross laughed. Then, realizing it wasn't a bad idea, he told her to leave it to him. Phyllis insisted she wanted to do it herself. Sandor hung up, then fired off a telegram: "Don't you realize your decisions are bound to be wrong?!" Phyllis ignored him.

She bought a set of Ordnance maps, and realized that to update them she had to do her own research. She set out every day on foot, walking London's streets, making notes, adding street numbers and subway stops, deleting streets that had disappeared. After putting in as long as eighteen hours a day, she would soak her sore feet and put her notes on cards indexed alphabetically. "So A-to-Z seemed to me the only

THE MAPMAKER AND HER BUSINESS

A MAP SAVED LONDON

Thematic maps put information into the context of a place. One thematic map of London is said to have saved people from a terrible disease known as cholera.

People knew the symptoms of cholera: giddiness, vomiting, raging headaches, and diarrhea like water, flecked with tiny bits of the victim's own intestinal lining. Some victims go into convulsions; others curl up in pain and have to be straightened out for burial. But how did cholera spread?

Dr. John Snow of London wasn't the first to suggest that contaminated water might be the cause of cholera. But he was the first to prove it. In 1849, he published a pamphlet saying that, if toilets of sick people were flushed into the water supply, healthy people would become infected. The Royal College of Physicians rejected his idea, saying, "No sufficient reasons have been found for adopting the theory."

In 1855, as London reeled from a new cholera epidemic, John Snow republished his pamphlet – this time, with a map. With black dashes it marked the houses where each of 616 cholera deaths had occurred in London's Soho district. Most of the black was clustered around the Broad Street pump. Near Soho's eleven other pumps, there were few or no black lines. Dr. Snow begged his neighbors to remove the Broad Street pump handle. Puzzled, they did so. From that day on, the cholera cases dwindled, then disappeared. Later, people learned that a cracked sewer pipe above the pump's well was leaking sewage into the water.

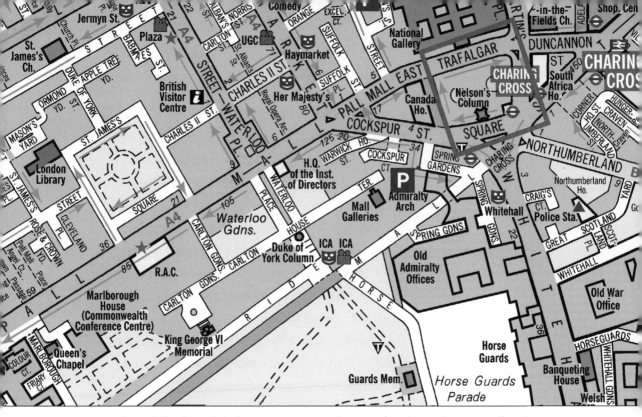

One day, Phyllis dropped the box of street names that started with T. *She ran to collect the cards, but one of them blew away and landed on the roof of a bus. When her first* London A–Z *was published, it was missing one of the most famous places in London, Trafalgar Square — shown here in the current* London A–Z.

possible title [for my book]," she later explained. Her father sent a telegram, ordering her to call her guide *The OK Map of London* instead. Phyllis paid no attention.

For more than a year she worked, retraining her artist's hand to draw streets with mathematical precision. Then she tracked down her parents' old Geographia employees and convinced them to help prepare her project for printing.

That first edition of *London A–Z* said on its cover, "Produced under the direction of Alexander Gross." Although her father had done no work and had given her no support, Phyllis loved the charming old scoundrel and wanted to honor him. Besides, he had a reputation as a mapmaker, and she didn't.

At first, Sandor's name failed to convince London booksellers to take her guidebook. Some turned Phyllis away because she was a woman. Others thought her book looked amateurish. One bookseller, a British Nazi, turned her away because he suspected she was Jewish.

Phyllis stubbornly pestered people to carry her guide. Booksellers who did found that it sold well, so they ordered more copies. When Sandor turned up unexpectedly in London, he was impressed to learn that his daughter's new business, the Geographer's A–Z Map Company, was showing a profit, and asked to be made a business partner. Flattered, Phyllis agreed. It wouldn't matter, she thought, since Sandor now lived in New York.

It was a big mistake. Back in the U.S., her father started pelting her with telegrams: "Consult me on every detail. . . . Do as I say!" When Phyllis reported that she had just placed a new order for a quarter-million copies of the A–Z, her father raged, "You have inherited your mother's recklessness! Don't expect me to get you out of trouble!"

By now it was 1939. Hitler's Nazi armies invaded Poland, and England went to war. Paper was in short supply, and the British government banned the making of maps that might be useful to Germans planning an invasion of England. The Geographer's A–Z Map Company closed down. As German bombs flattened London, Phyllis realized that the streets she had explored on foot were now choked with rubble. Whole neighborhoods were wiped off the map.

The war ended in 1945, and American soldiers flooding into the city got lost in its maze of streets and bombed-out neighborhoods. Suddenly everybody needed a guidebook again. Sandor decided he was the man to produce it. He came to London to exercise his rights as a partner in the business, and to force his daughter out. She'd be happier sticking to painting, he said.

Father and daughter had a terrible scene in a London restaurant. Then Sandor wrote to Phyllis's brother, saying that the Geographer's A–Z Map

The covers of early and current editions of London A–Z. *About 60 million copies have been sold since 1936.*

Company was too important to be left to a woman. "I therefore have no alternative than to give you control of the London business," Sandor told Tony, giving him his shares in the company. Tony had a wife and child to support, and accepted the offer. Phyllis was so shocked by her family's betrayal that she collapsed and went blind.

Now it was Sandor and Tony's turn for a shock. The A–Z employees said they had no intention of working for strangers who had never shown any interest in their work. They were going to stick by Phyllis. Sandor and Tony realized that the A–Z Company might collapse. They backed off.

After several months of rest, Phyllis regained her sight, forgave her father and her brother, and concentrated on rebuilding her company. It would be nice to report that the Gross family never fought again. Alas, Sandor couldn't help himself. In 1957, bankrupt yet again, he made one more attempt to gain control of the Geographer's A–Z Map Company. He telegraphed Phyllis that he was coming to London. The ever-optimistic Phyllis replied with a telegram that began, "Darling darling Papa, how we look forward to the joy of being with you . . . "

Sandor boarded the Queen Mary ocean liner with greed in his old heart, plotting to steal his daughter's profitable business. Aboard ship, somewhere in the mid-Atlantic, he died peacefully in his sleep. And the Geographer's A–Z Map Company kept growing.

Phyllis was a good boss. She hired people she trusted and let them get on with the job, while she headed off to paint and to visit friends all over the world. She told her godchildren to call her "Auntie Pig." But to her employees – her real family now – she was the legendary Mrs. P.

Her last public outing was in 1996. To celebrate the sixtieth anniversary of her company, she took more than 200 A–Z staff and their families to EuroDisney in France. As Phyllis, almost ninety, beamed from her wheelchair, her mapmaking family celebrated the fact that they had become one of the bestselling map publishers in the world, with more than 200 titles in their catalogue.

Maps are about gaining power over a landscape. But Phyllis Isobel Gross Pearsall was no conqueror or colony-founder. Her maps empowered ordinary people – tourists and Londoners alike – to find their way around a confusing city. They enabled Mrs. P to prove that a woman can make a fortune in business. And they showed that a kind heart and hard work can usually find a path through the tangled wilderness of one's own family.

THE MAPMAKERS' EYES

Mapping from Above

ON A WARM evening in 1966, Stewart Brand and some friends are sitting on a rooftop in San Francisco, gazing at the full moon. Nine years have passed since the Russians, and then the Americans, sent satellites into space. Tonight those satellites are probably up there, whirring across the dark sky. "Why," demands Brand, a free-thinking 1960s visionary, "Why haven't we seen a photograph of the whole Earth yet?"

His friends agree that such a picture should be taken from space. The next day they put the question on hundreds of buttons. Then they troop off to the public library and look up the addresses of every U.S. congressman and senator, and their secretaries, as well as the members of the Soviet Union's Politburo. Everyone is sent a button.

The trick works – Brand thinks the secretaries put on the buttons so the bosses had to pay attention. The pressure gets to NASA, the U.S. National Aeronautics and Space Administration, and the result is a photo taken by astronauts on the Apollo Seventeen mission. It appears on later editions of Brand's *The Whole Earth Catalog*, the hippie bible he publishes from 1968 until 1985.

On their way to the Moon, the Apollo Seventeen crew sent back this image of the whole Earth (or at least, its Mediterranean and African side). Asia is on the northeast horizon.

Photos taken from the sky are now a key mapmaking tool, helping to answer important questions: Are hurricanes coming? Are crops going to be bountiful enough to feed everyone? Are waterways

THE HIGHEST ART

From up high you can see a lot more than ever before. But how can you take what you see and translate it into mapmaking? In 1822, Frenchman Louis Daguerre came up with an invention to fix images of light and dark on chemically treated surfaces. Now we know his "daguerreotypes" much better as "photographs."

Taking a photograph from a balloon was not for the faint-hearted. The wicker basket suspended from the balloon where the photographer worked often swung wildly in the wind. To make things worse, in those days photographers used a "wet plate" technique that involved coating one side of a silver plate with a chemical solution immediately before use. Then, making sure the sticky plate was kept in complete darkness, the photographer plunged it into a silver nitrate solution to make it light-sensitive. Once the plate was exposed and the photograph taken, it had to be developed on the spot.

How could you do all that in a balloon? In 1857 a man named Gaspard Tournachon, known as Nadar, thought he could sort these problems out by taking aloft a lightproof blanket, and, keeping his chemicals and plates under the blanket, preparing his photo plates by feel. The first time he tried this complicated maneuver, he discovered that the hydrogenated sulfur fumes from his balloon's fuel desensitized his chemicals. The plates were all blank. So Nadar tried again, this time leaning away from the fumes and out of the basket to prepare his plates. On an autumn day in 1858, Nadar descended from his balloon ride with the world's first aerial photo: a pale portrait of three houses of a small village on the outskirts of Paris, so clear you could even see a policeman in the street.

becoming polluted? Are countries engaging in military buildups?

Of course, aerial photography hasn't replaced human-made maps. Human beings still have to judge how to label streets, mark political boundaries, and decide whether a line in a photograph is a road or a fence. What our eyes in the sky give us is a new range of powers.

They even equip us to map through time. Thanks to aerial photography, archaeologists can detect the outlines of structures built thousands of years ago. Photos of Stonehenge taken in the 1920s by English pilot O.G.S. Crawford revealed that the mysterious complex had once stretched in an avenue all the way to the Avon River. Aerial photos like Crawford's carry human perception to times and places where the human body cannot yet go. Humans haven't yet visited Mars, but thanks to color photos of the planet's surface taken in 1976 by the Viking spacecraft, we have scanned its distant tan-colored deserts.

Our first successful attempt to see the world from the sky dates back to when the Cassini family was mapping France. In June 1783, Joseph-Michel and Etienne Montgolfier sent up the first hot-air balloon (they got the idea from watching smoke rise up out of chimneys). Later that same year, on October 15, a daring young man named J.F. de Rozier stepped into a basket below a billowing balloon. The Montgolfier brothers loosened the ropes, and up he went. By stoking a small stove underneath the balloon's bottom opening, de Rozier was able to maintain a height of 24 meters (80 feet) for five minutes.

In 1859, the year after Nadar took the world's first aerial photo, a colonel in the French army, named Aimé Laussedat pioneered "photogrammetry," or photo-aided mapmaking. He came up with a combination of camera and theodolite and sent his invention aloft on a kite. Eventually he produced a map of Paris based on overlapping aerial photographs.

Aerial photographers had to deal with the fact that, if you look directly down at something, a house or a human, you see a square or a circle. Side views are needed to really make sense of the 3-D shape. At the

Artist Honoré Daumier sketched the fearless photographer Nadar taking photos of Paris from his balloon. The artist joked that Nadar had made photography "the highest art."

end of the 19th century, Theodore Schimpflug developed a special aerial camera with eight lenses. Why so many? The center lens pointed directly down, and the others pointed at angles to give those crucial side views.

Despite these advances, photo-mapping from balloons was awkward simply because balloons were hard to steer. Then, 120 years after the Montgolfier brothers launched humankind skywards, two American brothers, Orville and Wilbur Wright, invented the airplane.

In some ways, taking photos from these first fragile planes was even more hair-raising than leaning out of balloons. Sometimes the photos were snapped by the pilot, who, while trying to keep his rickety machine aloft, would pull a cord attached to a camera fixed to the plane's struts. Sometimes the photos were taken by a passenger lying face-down with the camera pointed through a hole in the cockpit floor. These were open cockpits, so photographers had to change each photographic plate with fingers clumsy from the freezing cold.

Then came World War I. Germans used zeppelins to take photos of enemy positions; the Allies sent up kite-balloons with cameras attached to snap fortifications at places like Vimy Ridge. These photo-maps proved invaluable for the Canadian troops' successful assault on Vimy Ridge in 1917.

After World War I, the Australians and Americans began to use aerial photography to complement their geographical surveys. But it was in big, empty Canada that aerial mapping really made sense. In 1919, with surplus warplanes donated by the British, the Canadian government established an Air Board for aerial surveys and started to map places it had been too costly — and just too far — to go before.

Throughout the 1920s, little planes buzzed across the bush and beyond the timberline. Even in summer, it was cold. One pilot who leaned out of his cockpit to admire the view reported that being hit by oncoming ice pellets felt like being "hit full in the face with a hammer."

The planes in those days weren't pressurized, and mostly flew at an altitude of 1500 meters (5,000 feet). That meant it was far more effective to take oblique, or side-angled, photos of the lands that stretched on either side of the plane, rather than just the thin strip directly beneath. So Air Board cartographers figured out how to transfer the oblique photos onto a perspective grid and then straighten out the grid. Now serious maps could be made from the thousands of photos flooding into the Air Board and the Topographical Survey of Canada offices. By 1924, the pilots had covered 103,000 km² (40,000 square miles) with their cameras. In 1925, the Canadian government issued its first official map based on oblique-view aerial photographs. Before long, Canada was the first country to be completely photographed from the air.

Lumber, hydro, and oil companies also wanted maps. But there

DEFEATING THE RED BARON

World War I's most legendary pilot was Germany's Baron Manfred von Richthofen, known as the Red Baron because he painted the sides of his Fokker tri-plane a bright red. By 1918, the twenty-five-year-old had shot down eighty Allied planes – most of them slow-moving reconnaissance planes scouting and taking photos.

On the morning of April 21, 1918, the Red Baron spotted the No. 3 Australian Squadron observation planes over the fields of northern France. They were guarded by a team of Sopwith Camel planes led by Roy Brown, a Canadian in Britain's Royal Air Force. That morning Brown was also keeping a special eye on his high-school buddy, Wilfrid "Wop" May, on his first combat mission.

Brown told May to stay out of the dogfights, but May couldn't resist firing at the German Fokkers. Then his guns jammed and he decided to head back to British lines. The Red Baron spotted May's plane breaking away, and gave chase. Roy Brown saw his friend in trouble and swooped down. The three planes screamed low over the French fields, sometimes just above treetop height, and then crossed into British airspace. Australian Gunner 3801, Robert Buie, took aim at the Fokker. So did Roy Brown, closing in from behind.

The Fokker crashed, the Red Baron slumped over his control panel. Some Canadians claim that Brown shot down the Red Baron; the Australians will tell you Buie did it. But no one disputes that the terrifying morning only intensified a passion for flying in May and Brown, who went on to become legends as bush pilot explorers and surveyors of the Canadian north.

weren't many maps of regions like the Mackenzie River delta or the area east of Lake Athabaska — a region bigger than all of Europe — then known as the Barrens. No one could survey such a place on foot. Even Inuit hunters could hardly eke a living from the empty landscape. But former fighter pilots like Roy Brown were desperate for an excuse to climb back into their cockpits. They started bush pilot companies to survey the land from the air, and to fly in geologists into the wilderness to stake claims.

In September 1929, Colonel C. MacAlpine of the Dominion Explorers Club and his crew set off from Winnipeg to survey and prospect in the Barrens. But clouds of smoke from distant forest fires obscured the explorers' view, and strong winds blew them way off course. They touched down on a big lake that turned out to be near the Arctic Ocean. The Inuit family who found them said that the closest help was at the Hudson's Bay Company post at Cambridge Bay on Victoria Island. Without enough fuel to fly out, the men realized that they would have to walk. As soon as the ice got more solid, the Inuit said they would guide them across the frozen sea to Cambridge Bay. The group set out in November. But the ice was still thin and, as they trudged forward, an Inuit mother carrying a baby stepped right through. To save herself and her child, she lay face-down, spreading her weight until the others could pull her and her child to safety and dry clothes. Finally the group spotted the Maude, a Hudson's Bay Company ship. Between them and the ship lay 5 kilometers (3 miles) of bad ice. The Inuit said they would have to dash across to keep ahead of its cracks. And so they ran for their lives — men, women, dogs, and Dominion Club explorers.

Worried about the missing explorers, flying ace Roy Brown and other bush pilots spent the autumn searching for them. On November 4, the rescuers heard via ship's radio that the explorers were safely aboard the Maude. They picked up the lost expedition and headed home. En route,

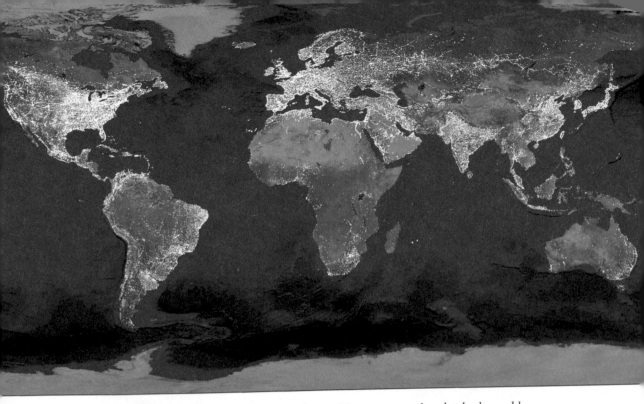

This NASA photograph shows city lights across the globe. You can see how bright the wealthy cities of Europe and America are. The interiors of Africa, Australia, and South America are darker. They are regions with few people — and few who can afford bright lights.

at a refueling stop, the wing of Brown's plane snapped off and he crash-landed in a snow bank. The others flew on, leaving him wounded and sheltering in his mangled plane. It was a week before the rescuer was rescued.

World War II halted the golden age of bush pilot mapping. After the war's end, America and the Soviet Union faced each other across the ruins of Europe as new Cold War enemies. The race for technological and military superiority began. In 1955, the U.S. announced that it would soon have rockets capable of launching a satellite into orbit. The Soviets beat them to it with the launch, on October 4, 1957, of an 83-kilogram (184-pound) satellite called Sputnik.

Sputnik made the Western powers panic. U.S. Senate majority leader Lyndon Johnson, who later became president, warned, "The Roman

Empire controlled the world because it could build roads. . . . The British Empire was dominant because it had ships. In the air age, we were powerful because we had airplanes. Now the Communists have established a foothold in outer space."

Worse, foreign satellites could look down and see what the Americans were doing. In fact, they could look anywhere. In 1959, the Soviet satellite Luna sent back never-before-seen images of the far side of the Moon.

The space race was on. Through the 1960s, America's Lunar Orbiter satellites surveyed 99 percent of the Moon, in order to scout out a landing site for the spaceship Apollo Eleven. Mapmaking was now officially off the Earth and into the rest of the Solar System.

Because the Apollo's four-legged landing craft needed a level surface, the mission planners had to have detailed maps. Carefully made from satellite photographs, these maps were able to pinpoint the perfect landing place at Tranquility Base, lunar coordinates 0 degrees 41 minutes north, and 23 degrees 25 minutes east. That was where, on June 20, 1969, the first human beings touched down, and astronaut Neil Armstrong announced from another world, "The Eagle has landed."

Since then there have been more spacecraft, whose names sound like a roll call of history's greatest explorers, cartographers, and ships: Viking, Magellan, Galileo, Challenger, Cassini-Huygens.

While they have peered into space, other craft have stared down at the Earth. The U.S. government's LANDSAT of the 1970s was a stubby-winged satellite that surveyed our home planet from 900 kilometers (560 miles) up. Using multi-spectrum scanners (blue, green, red, and near infra-red), it transmitted the images to the ground at a scale of 1:500,000.

LANDSAT created a revolution in mapmaking. It forced mapmakers to correct maps of Antarctica and to reposition remote islands. It showed images that let us diagnose our planet's problems: urban sprawl, damaged crops, and the destruction of the Amazon rainforest.

MAPPING THE UNIVERSE

Ever since her father, a chemist, showed Margaret Geller a snowflake under a microscope, she wanted to be a scientist. She decided to devote her life to what she has called "the modest goal" of "mapping the visible universe."

In the early 1980s, Geller and fellow astronomer John Huchra were working at the Smithsonian Center for Astrophysics, located in Cambridge, Massachusetts. They started measuring the distances and positions of more than 10,000 galaxies – vast clusters of stars, like our own Milky Way – in the sky above Earth's northern hemisphere. Then they asked one of their graduate students, Valerie de Lapparent, to feed all these positions into a computer and calculate their distribution.

Geller expected to find that galaxies were evenly distributed all over the universe, like falling snow. What she found instead was astonishing. "Galaxies appear on thin surfaces around vast dark regions, like soap bubbles 200 million light years across," she later told a group of female university students. Scientists refer to the edge of these bubbles as a Great Wall. And great it is – the "thin" line where there is a concentration of galaxies is nearly 20 million light-years thick.

Astronomers peering into the southern sky have since found a Southern Wall of galaxies too. And beyond those walls? Almost nothing. Geller and her colleagues have made three-dimensional maps, and some people say these maps of the limitless universe remind them of something you see everyday – soap foam.

The latest generation of surveillance satellites — American, French, and Israeli, as well as private industry satellites — can now "map" objects as small as a human being lying lengthwise on a beach towel.

As aerial photographs change our perception of where we are, they change our consciousness of who we are — just as Stewart Brand, gazing at the sky that night in San Francisco, suspected would happen. One shift in consciousness came with the Apollo spacecraft images — the whole Earth, and Earthrise from the Moon. They let us see ourselves as others might see us . . . if there's anyone else out there.

Nothing has ever driven home our planet's uniqueness — and aloneness — as powerfully as these views of Earth from space. The images confirm what people have probably suspected ever since they looked around them — ever since they made the first attempts to map the difference between Here and There.

They confirm that Earth is marvelous, and that it is spinning through a vast and still-uncharted universe. Out there, there are billions of stories to tell.

Acknowledgments

I'd like to thank my publisher, Kathy Lowinger, for having the idea for this book, and for giving it her all-important commitment, humor, and good taste. Thanks, too, to Kat Mototsune, for her painstaking editorial work on many versions of the text, her sleuthing for images, and her patience with my computer-related illiteracy.

Ed Dahl, the former early cartography specialist at the National Archives of Canada, and a legend among cartographic historians, was kind enough to read the manuscript and warn me off grandiose and unqualified claims, as well as misplaced modifiers. Conrad Heidenreich, professor emeritus of geography, York University, offered crucial enthusiasm and encouragement; he was also generous with my queries and corrected many errors (those that remain are mine and no one else's).

John Fraser and Anna Luengo at Massey College, University of Toronto, know how important Massey has been to me, as well as to so many other writers. Thanks to Richard Landon at the Thomas Fisher Rare Book Library for showing me some of its treasures, and to Jacqueline Krikorian, a friend from Massey, for her hospitality in Washington when I visited the Library of Congress.

Thanks as well to Cliff Thornton of the Captain Cook Society (www.captaincooksociety.com), and to Dr. Anthony Rice of The Challenger Society (www.challenger-society.org.uk/) for their advice.

I should also acknowledge debts to John Noble Wilford's superb book *The Mapmakers*, Daniel Boorstin's *The Discoverers*, and *The British Library Companion to Maps and Mapmaking*.

FURTHER READING

Chapter 1

The Discoverers by Daniel J. Boorstin; Vintage Books, New York, 1983.
This book has two chapters on the Norse voyages, and Freydis too.

"Turbulent Priest Forged Viking Map of America"; *Times of London*,
    08/04/02.
The story of the Vinland Map forgery.

Proceedings of the Vinland Map Conference, Washburn, ed.; University of
    Chicago Press, Chicago, 1971.
For the worms and so on.

Chapter 2

The Kingdom in the Sun, by John Julius Norwich; Longman's, London, 1970.
For more on Roger II of Sicily.

The History of Cartography, Vol II, David Woodward, ed.; University of
    Chicago Press, 1992.
For more on al-Idrisi.

Chapter 3

When China Ruled the Seas: The Treasure Fleet of the Dragon Throne,
    by Louise Levathes; Oxford University Press, New York
    and Oxford, 1994.
Still the best book on Chinese exploration in Cheng Ho's time.

Chapter 4

Prince Henry the Navigator, by John Ure; Constable, London, 1970.
    For all ages.

Prince Henry 'The Navigator': A Life, by Peter Russell; Yale University Press,
    New Haven and London, 2001.
A more critical look at Henry, written for adult readers.

Chapter 5

Mercator, The Man Who Mapped the Planet, by Nicholas Crane; Weidenfeld & Nicolson, London, 2002.

Chapter 6

La carte de Cassini: l'extraordinaire aventure de la carte de France, by Monique Pelletier; Presses de l'Ecole nationale des Ponts et Chaussées, Paris, 1990.
In French.

The Mapmakers, by John Noble Wilford; Vintage Books, New York, 1981, revised 2001.

Chapter 7

Captain James Cook, by Richard Hough; W.W. Norton & Co., New York and London, 1994.

Longitude, The True Story of a Lone Genius Who Solved the Greatest Scientific Problem of his Time, by Dava Sobel; Walker & Co., New York, 1995.
Highly recommended.

Chapter 8

Lewis and Clark, by Dayton Duncan; Alfred A. Knopf, New York, 1997.
For more on the Corps of Discovery.

Sources of the River: Tracking David Thompson Across Western North America, by Jack Nisbet; Sasquatch Books, Seattle, 1994.
For more on David Thompson.

Where is Here? Canada's Maps and the Stories They Tell, by Alan Marantz; Penguin Canada, Toronto, 2002.
For more on First Nations maps.

Chapter 9

South America Called Them, by Victor Wolfgang von Hagen; Alfred A. Knopf, New York, 1945.

Chapter 10

The Edge of an Unfamiliar World, by Susan Schlee; E.P. Dutton, New York, 1973.
General oceanography.

Chapter 11

Trespassers on the Roof of the World, by Peter Hopkirk; John Murray, London, 1982.

The Forbidden Frontiers, The Survey of India from 1765–1949, by Showell Styles; Hamish Hamilton, London, 1970.

Chapter 12

Mrs. P's Journey, by Sarah Hartley; Simon & Schuster, London, 2001.

Fleet Street, Tite Street, Queer Street, by Phyllis Pearsall; self-published, London, 1983.
Phyllis's autobiography.

King Cholera: The Biography of Disease, by Norman Longmate; Hamish Hamilton, London, 1966.
For more on Dr. John Snow.

Chapter 13

Aerial Photography, by Grover Heiman; The Macmillan Co., Collier Macmillan, New York, 1972.

Skyview Canada, by Don W. Thomson; Dept. of Energy Mines and Resources, Ottawa, 1975.

The Bush Pilots: a pictorial history of a Canadian phenomenon, by J. A. Foster; McClelland & Stewart, Toronto, 1990.

The Right Stuff, by Tom Wolfe; Farrar, Straus, Giroux, New York, 1979.
For space exploration.

Pale Blue Dot: A vision of the human future in space, by Carl Sagan; Random House, New York, 1994.

INDEX

PHOTO CREDITS

Cover: Africa, from the *Catalan Atlas*: John Webb/The Art Archive

Page

2 Hondius world map: Courtesy of Library of Congress, Geography & Map Division

4 Vinland Map: Beinecke Rare Book and Manuscript Library, Yale University

9 Babylonian world map: © The British Museum

13 Illuminated manuscript: Burgerbibliothek Bern, Cod. 120. II f.96r

16 Map from Claudius Ptolemy, *Cosmographia*: Courtesy of Library of Congress, Geography & Map Division

18 Al-Idrisi world map: Bodleian Library, University of Oxford, Bodleian Image: MS. Pococke 375 folios 3v–4r

23 Huang He Wan Li Tu (Pictorial Map of Yellow River): Courtesy of Library of Congress, Asian Division

26 Stamps: Courtesy of Dan's Topical Stamps, http://sio.midco.net/danstopicalstamps

39 Africa, from the *Catalan Atlas*: John Webb/The Art Archive

41 Statue of Henry the Navigator: © Dave G. Houser/CORBIS/MAGMA

47 Mercator polar map: Library and Archives of Canada, NMC-16097 (photo by Conrad Heidenreich)

51 Portrait of Mercator and Hondius: Stewart Museum at the Fort, Montreal (photo by Conrad Heidenreich)

53 Carte de France: Cliché Bibliothèque nationale de France, Paris

56 The Landing of Jacques Cartier/Vallard Chart: Mary Evans Picture Library

61 Portrait of Cassini I: Cliché Bibliothèque nationale de France, Paris

63 Kealakekua Bay, Hawaii: Dr. James P. McVey/ NOAA (National Oceanic and Atmospheric Administration)

120 Map from *London A–Z*: Reproduced by permission of Geographers' A–Z Map Co. Ltd. © Crown Copyright 2003. All rights reserved. Licence number 100017302.

122 *London A–Z* covers: Reproduced by permission of Geographers' A–Z Map Company

125 Earth from space: Courtesy of NASA

132 City lights from space: Courtesy of NASA/JPL/Caltech